THE
WAY
WE
GARDEN
NOW

THE WAY WE GARDEN NOW

41 PICK-AND-CHOOSE PROJECTS FOR PLANTING YOUR PARADISE LARGE OR SMALL

KATHERINE WHITESIDE

ILLUSTRATIONS BY PETER GERGELY

CLARKSON POTTER/PUBLISHERS

New York

All rights reserved.
Published in the United States by Clarkson Potter/Publishers,
an imprint of the Crown Publishing Group,
a division of Random House, Inc., New York.
www.crownpublishing.com
www.clarksonpotter.com

Clarkson N. Potter is a trademark and Potter and colophon
are registered trademarks of Random House, Inc.

Library of Congress Cataloging-in-Publication Data
    Whiteside, Katherine
    The way we garden now: 41 pick-and-choose projects for
planting your paradise large or small / Katherine Whiteside.—1st ed.
    1. Gardening   I. Title
    SB450.97.W48 2007
    635—dc22   2006017793

ISBN 978-0-307-35135-7

Printed in Spain

DESIGN BY MARYSARAH QUINN

10 9 8 7 6 5 4 3 2 1

First Edition

TO *Dean, Joe, Micah, and August*
—KW

TO *Val, Ben, Page, and my wonderful family*
—PG

THANKS TO THE FOLLOWING FOR THEIR HELP WITH THIS BOOK: *Nina Collins, Elissa Altman, Marysarah Quinn, Doris Cooper, Lauren Shakely, Matthew Elblonk, Selina Cicogna, Rita Riehle, Diane Phillips, and Vic Carlson, RIP*

TABLE OF CONTENTS

I. GET GOING:
BEGIN WITH THE BASICS

II. KEEP GOING:
GET OVER YOUR DESIGN DILEMMAS

III. GET GROWING:
ORGANIZE YOUR ORNAMENTALS

IV. KEEP GROWING: ADD EDIBLES IN INCREMENTS

V. KEEP ON GOING AND NEVER STOP GROWING: CELEBRATE THE SEASONS

PREFACE

THIS IS NOT YOUR MOM'S GARDEN BOOK. Nothing against your mom, but just as we have changed the way we arrange our houses, do our work, cook our meals, imagine our families, get our exercise, and spend our spare time, we nesters have changed the way America gardens. The forever-unattainable goal of "perfection" is a relic of the past, and I am here to yell "whoopee!" with all of the rest of you out there who want to make sure that pleasure is a permanent part of your darling domestic scene. Forget making a perfect garden. Instead, let's talk about having a perfectly enjoyable garden.

This book is for anyone who wishes to have a garden. It is for absolute beginners, for moderately begun gardeners, and for those who feel that their existing gardens need a bit of beautifying. I promise to show any ordinary person with normal skill levels how to begin or embellish the garden of their dreams.

The Way We Garden Now addresses all of America's gardening regions. I have had gardens in Zones 5, 6, 7, in southwestern England, and am now learning how to garden long-distance, part-time in Pasadena, California. A big part of my work constantly takes me to other parts of the country, and I'll tell you this: Everyone everywhere is loving their garden. A garden can mean a New York rooftop, a Chicago townhouse space, an Atlanta allotment, a Missouri farm, an L.A. cliffhanger, or a borrowed churchyard in Portland, Maine. Americans have changed the way we want to garden, but, wow, we are ever wanting to garden.

The 41 pick-and-choose projects here show you how to put your energy, enthusiasm, and individuality into good honest effort that will start rewarding you as soon as you begin. I hope to inspire your garden dreams by telling you up front what the payoff is for each project. Then I will help you get organized for action. I give you a list of things you'll need to purchase before you start and a list of simple tools to have at the ready for work. The how-to part of each project is written like a recipe with numbered steps so that you can start and stop work as needed. Hey, life is big and interruptions always happen.

Gardening can become a normal, creative part of your life if you don't worry too much about the whole process. I mean, when was the last time you read the entire newspaper without an interruption? Gardening is not a race to the finish line; it is an enjoyable amble through your own private paradise. The process of creating a garden should be as rewarding and satisfying as the end result.

Over the years, I have done all of the projects I describe in *The Way We Garden Now*. I am a hands-on gardener with a healthy disregard for fancy tools, an aversion to overspending, and no time to recover from extreme exhaustion. Paying too much money and spending too much time on your garden will leave you feeling worse for wear and, in the end, won't help you to have a better garden. As you work with the projects outlined here, keep checking the dial on your pleasure meter and, when it runs low, stop and get yourself a cool drink and a comfy lawn chair. Sit, sip, admire the work you have accomplished, and promise yourself that you won't start again until you really feel like it. This is how I garden, and I end up getting a lot done with no anger-management issues.

The Way We Garden Now is a new-style primer for a new generation. Use it as a guide to discovering your inner creativity, strength, and, yep, peace of mind. Now get out there, get going, get growing, and have a great garden!

I.

GET GOING: BEGIN WITH THE BASICS

The first section of *The Way We Garden Now* will get you going on the path to happy gardening. These ten projects level the playing field between beginners and those who have already begun, but whether you are starting a garden from scratch or somewhere further along, this section forms the foundation for a pleasant ongoing garden experience. And, to start you off on the right foot, here's a secret tip: Ceaselessly fretting over having a perfect garden is not fun, but getting out there and accomplishing basic garden goals will always leave you happily fulfilled.

If you do not yet have a garden, don't despair: Every one of us has been in the same predicament you're in now. Whether they have a brand-new patch of bulldozed soil, a rehab draped with years of weeds, or even a pristine but boring expanse of lawn, all beginner gardeners ask the same question: "Where in the heck do I start?" This section solves that basic problem in ten easy, manageable projects that will turn your yard into a working garden.

If you already have a garden, then you know very well that gardening is a continuing process. You probably learned years ago that the best way to improve your garden is to read what works for other people and to constantly apply that information to your own space. Even the most seasoned gardener can hit a glitch on the path to garden happiness. Some seasons my garden has gotten embarrassingly out of hand, but if I return to the basic tasks outlined in this section, I can whip everything back into shape without wasting too much time despairing over "Where in the heck do I start?"

Because, yes, my friend, no matter where you are in gardening years, there will always be the need to pay your respects to the basic foundation skills. Here are the projects that will teach you, or remind you, how to build your happy garden.

The first four projects describe the cornerstones you need to begin gardening.

The next four projects explain how to master four basic garden chores.

The final two foundation projects deal with wildlife that can enhance or destroy your gardening efforts.

ONE

MAKE A NEW BED

WHAT'S THE PAYOFF?

This medium-sized project gleefully explains a smart way to make a new bed, with no digging or rototilling required. It is the key to your garden's beginning and to its expansion. Often the only stumbling block between a brilliant idea and end results is the daunting prospect of digging up expanses of lawn or weeds to create new beds.

Every gardener eventually faces the challenge of creating new beds for flowers, vegetables, a cutting garden, or an herb patch. Clearing sod is also necessary when installing a patio or paths. If you have ever tried to dig up large areas of lawn, you know that this is very, very difficult and dirty work. Traditional methods leave compacted soil that must be redug and reworked before planting. *(See "Removing Turf the Hard Way," page 16.)* Although I am sure that there is a rototiller fan club out there, in my opinion, this method is very difficult and dirty. Mechanically churning turf leaves a heaved-up mess full of weeds chopped into zillions of sproutable pieces.

The way I make a new bed has a longer time line, but my "Savvy

Way" is so gentle that even people with terrible backs can make smooth, weed-free, easily cultivated beds. Although most enthusiastic gardeners are always ready for some garden action, we are also really smart about how we do things.

The "Savvy Way" involves smothering and solarizing lawn and weeds into nothingness. It is ecologically sound and an approved organic technique. This project can be begun at any time of year and will take several months to produce a new bed. If the timing works for you, autumn is a great period to begin this project because the process occurs over the winter and, when spring arrives, you'll be good to go.

This is the way that I always make a new bed, so it is referenced repeatedly throughout this book. It's how I made my potager, increased the ornamental areas, and began special beds for cutting, for irises, and to make a sunflower folly. Once you see how easy this is, your gardening pleasure will increase as your garden area does.

REMOVING TURF THE HARD WAY

If the area you want to clear is very small or if you are really impatient, you can remove the turf by hand. You will need a cheap steak knife, a sharpened spade, very strong arms, and a sturdy back. Use the steak knife to cut a square about 1 x 1 foot in the turf. Use the sharpened spade to lever under the grass and lift up the sod with the roots attached. This will include about three inches of topsoil. Using your hands, peel the square back and away. Pile this heavy piece into your garden cart and repeat until you really hurt and ache all over. Ugh, ugh, ugh.

PURCHASE PRIOR TO INSTALLATION

- Woven weed barrier cloth: enough to cover new bed area
- Mulch hay or straw: enough to cover and disguise the weed barrier

TOOLS

- Lawn mower or weed whacker
- Old newspapers
- Stakes and string
- Hose and nozzle

INSTALLATION

1. Using the stakes and string, lay out the perimeter of your new bed. Remember that flowers, herbs, and vegetables need plenty of sun. In general, a small herb bed can be 8 feet square, a sunflower folly 35 feet square, and a manageable vegetable potager somewhere in between. Plot flower beds so that they are wide enough to allow layers of plants from front to back.

2. Adjust the lawn mower blade to the lowest possible setting and mow the grass inside the perimeter as short as possible. If using a weed whacker, perform a military buzz cut. There's no need to remove the cuttings, as they will disappear soon enough.

3. Use the hose and nozzle to water the area thoroughly.

4. Cover this area with a thick layer of old newspapers. Entire sections can be used in one spot.

5. Water again. Saturate the newspapers to make them heavy and flat.

6. Stomp on top of the soggy papers to press them close to the soil. Water again if necessary.

7. Unroll the woven weed barrier and cover the soggy newspapers in long, overlapping pieces. Weigh down the edges with stones, logs, or bricks. Place a few weights in the middle and on the overlapping edges to keep the wind from displacing the fabric.

    OPTIONAL: Cover the weed barrier with a layer of mulch hay or straw. Water and stomp down to compact this top layer and help prevent it from blowing away.

8. Walk away. You are finished. The bed will make itself. (I wish the beds inside my house would do this.) The smothering action of the

WHAT IS WOVEN WEED BARRIER CLOTH?

Woven weed barrier cloth is made from very thin strips of strong black plastic woven into durable fabric. Woven weed barrier allows water to permeate, but it blocks sunlight and traps heat. It can be cut with ordinary scissors. Plastic sheeting is sometimes sold as weed barrier, but it is not recommended; the plastic, which looks just like the stuff used to make big garbage bags, shreds fairly quickly. While more expensive, woven weed barrier can be reused for many years. I still use pieces that are a decade old.

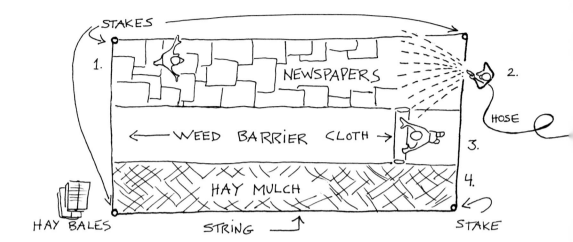

MULCH HAY OR STRAW

The mulch hay is only necessary if the aesthetics of a big black square waiting out there bothers you. Personally, I like the look of mulch hay or straw and do use these as cover-up on my weed barrier. I do not recommend substituting wood bark chips for hay in this project. Bark chips will not compact and end up blowing all over your garden. They do not decompose easily and are dangerous during summer's lawn mowing.

weed barrier and the heat of the sun (even in winter) will slowly but surely destroy all the grass, weeds, and weed seeds underneath.

9. After about 1 or 2 months, check under the layers to see if your new bed is clean and ready for planting. You should find bare soil with no evidence of growth. Magically, the tilth will be fine so that further working is unnecessary. You will probably also find many earthworms, since they will have been attracted to this warm, protected area. In spring and summer, this project may take 1 to 2 months for completion. Hot weather speeds action. An autumn-made bed will be ready for early-spring planting.

10. When the bed is ready to plant, fork the mulch hay or straw onto the compost pile. Roll up and store the weed barrier for future reuse. Remove

newspapers and allow them to dry before recycling them or burning them on a rubbish pile.

11. If this new bed is for flowers or vegetables, add old manure and
compost if you have it. You don't need to dig it in; just scratch it
into the surface with a standing cultivator or garden rake.

12. If this will be an herb bed, do not fertilize or use manure here.
Herbs are tastiest when grown in poor (or "lean") soil. Enriched soil
encourages lush growth to the detriment of herb flavors. *(See "Have
Some Herbs," page 223.)*

TWO

CREATE A COMPOST PILE

WHAT'S THE PAYOFF?

This small project shows you how to build and maintain a compost pile and explains what to do with the results. A compost pile will give you a place to recycle kitchen scraps and garden debris into well-balanced, slow-release, 100-percent-safe organic fertilizer. Compost will improve your soil, provide almost all the potting soil you'll require, and kick-start your organic gardening skill level.

Many gardeners avoid composting because it seems a bit difficult and fussy. This great little project describes "cold" composting. A cold compost pile takes longer than a "hot" (i.e., fussy) pile. A hot pile has specific ingredients, layered in specific ways, and is turned and worked over constantly. It transforms rubbish into compost very quickly, but requires lots of attention. A cold pile accepts ingredients as you have them and it does all its own work.

A cold pile works more slowly than a hot pile, but a normal family of four can easily produce enough compostables to keep both a "receivables" pile and a "working" pile going. By having these twin piles, you will be able to keep adding fresh materials to one pile while the other one works. For convenience, make pairs of compost piles (receivables and working) near the kitchen door, next to the vegetable garden, hidden near the flower borders, and off in the woods. Busy gardeners are often pressed for time, so it's necessary to make those dumping areas convenient.

PURCHASE PRIOR TO INSTALLATION

- 6 garden stakes, 4 feet tall
- 10 bales of hay
  or Inexpensive lattice, 3-feet-high strips, 20 feet long
  or 1 roll chicken wire
  or 1 roll snow fence
- 1 cheap stockpot with lid
- 1 large bag of manure
  or 1 small bag alfalfa meal
  or 1 small bag Litter Green kitty litter
  or 1 small bag rabbit chow pellets
- Black weed barrier cloth, 5 square feet

TOOLS

- Hand saw for cutting lattice
  or Wire cutters for cutting chicken wire or snow fence
- Mallet for pounding stakes

INSTALLATION

1. Choose the best location. A good rule of thumb is that you want your pile to be close enough to be convenient, yet tucked away enough to be discreet. Compost is the end result, but, basically, we are talking about garbage here.
2. Create a framework for a twin compost pile. Your rectangular pile

should be about 8 feet long and 5 feet wide with side-by-side twin compartments. One long side will be solid and the other completely open. The short ends and middle divider will be solid. The pile will be disguised more effectively if the open long end faces away from the garden or house.

3. Pound in garden stakes to make two 4-foot squares with a common middle. Set four hay bales end to end in a long straight line to form the long closed side. At one end, place a bale at a right angle and add one more bale in line with that to form a short, closed end. Repeat on the other end. Divide this space in the middle with two more bales of hay parallel to the ends. You should end up with two squares with one open side. The garden stakes will keep the hay bales from moving around during freezing weather. *Or* attach desired lattice or fencing to stake arrangement to make same twin compartment shape.

4. Your compost bins are ready for action.

5. Keep the lidded stockpot in the kitchen to collect "inside the

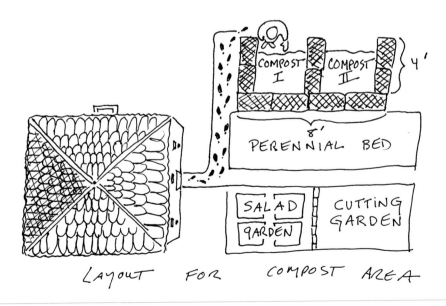

LAYOUT FOR COMPOST AREA

house" scraps. *(See "Inside Ingredients," at right)* When the pot is full, take it outside and dump into the left side of your twin compost bin.

6. "Outside the house" compost ingredients can be tossed in whenever you like. *(See "Outside Ingredients," at right)*

7. Scavenge biodegradable ingredients to add to your pile. Some quick suggestions are: manure (especially horse, cow, rabbit, sheep, and the dirty water from the goldfish bowl), hair from the pet groomer, and your own hair trimmings.

8. Do *not* put the following in the compost: sawdust from treated wood, weeds, diseased plants, used kitty litter, or dog doo.

9. When you have made a lumpy pile that is at least 3 feet square and tall, you can declare this side your "working pile." Dump a couple of handfuls of alfalfa pellets, clean Litter Green, pelletized rabbit chow, or manure on top to kick-start the action.

10. Water the pile liberally.

11. Cover with weed barrier cloth to retain warmth. (Water and warmth aid the decay process.) If you live in a dry climate, place a rock or brick in the middle of the cloth to make a depression that allows water to drip into the pile. If it is wet where you live, mound the pile so that excess water runs off. (Too much water makes the pile smell bad.)

12. Begin adding new compost material to the right-hand bin (your new receivables) and leave the working pile alone.

13. The compost in the left bin is ready (think months, not weeks) when you peek under the cloth and see

INSIDE INGREDIENTS

Acceptable ingredients for your compost pile include: coffee grounds, tea bags, egg shells, vegetable scraps, flour, sour milk, pet hair, onion skins, leftover dough, moldy yogurt, water from cooking vegetables, rice and other cereals, old salad, vacuum cleaner dust, and anything else biodegradable that doesn't have meat in it. Despite widespread advice out there not to, we compost our salad dressings and all dairy products with no adverse effects.

OUTSIDE INGREDIENTS

Since slow composting has no rules for layering ingredients, you can add garden debris as you have it. This may include: autumn leaves chopped up with the lawn mower, annual and perennial clippings and border rubbish, grass cuttings, bolted lettuces, rhubarb foliage, carrot tops, old wood shavings, wool (your entire old ragged gardening sweater will compost), sprinkles of wood ash, cornstalks, seaweed, and washed seashells.

WEEKEND PILE

If you garden primarily on weekends at another house, freeze your scraps to take to the country later. When you get there, dump the frozen mass onto your working pile.

mostly dark crumbly soil instead of chunks o' junk. Many people sift their compost, but I skip this little nicety. Just scoop up the good stuff (an old plastic nursery pot makes a great scoop) and throw any uncooked chunks right over into the receivables. Use your compost, now officially black gold, as described below.

USE YOUR COMPOST

Spread compost over new or existing beds, borders, and the vegetable potager. There is no need to dig in compost; just let it perk down from the surface.

When you transplant plants, add a dash of compost to the hole. It won't burn like commercial fertilizer.

Use compost when sowing tiny seeds. "Draw" a shallow drill with a pointy stick, carefully dribble in a line of water, scatter seeds into the drill, and cover with a line of fine compost. Pat firmly into place.

Use compost to replace storebought potting soil. Your plants will be stronger and less prone to disease.

Add a cup of compost to a 5-gallon bucket of water to make compost tea. Stir until dissolved and let steep for five days. This can be used to water indoor and outdoor plants.

THREE

DON'T BE A TOOL FOOL

WHAT'S THE PAYOFF?

Experienced gardeners know that tools can be seductive. They wink at you from store displays. They promise you a better life. They seem like a good idea at the time. But, in the end, an unused tool speaks of an impulsive, expensive mistake. This small project gives you a basic inventory of tools that are likely to become your faithful helpers. It also shows you how to organize these trusted friends so they are always there when you need them.

I am an enthusiastic amateur gardener, so I purchase and treat tools accordingly. To give you some insight into what this means, I also consider myself an enthusiastic amateur cook. In my small, lovable kitchen, I have a regular, domestic-use, low-cost stove, and a fridge and dishwasher from Sears. I do not use a microwave, food processor, or big mixer because I enjoy the taste, feel, and smell of the cooking process. I have funky old knives that I sharpen haphazardly, an assortment of cast-iron skillets, some odd pots and pans, and a few mixing bowls. In other words, my kitchen tools aren't fancy, but they are more than adequate to create delicious meals. My garden tools follow along that same line.

You can buy all the tools in the world and still have no garden. Better to spend money on plants and use your leftover cash to buy what you need to take care of them. Here is the inventory of tools that I own and use. The how-to part of this project is how to store all this stuff.

INVENTORY

HAND TOOLS

- Trowels: 2 (a good-quality and sturdy one for extensive bulb planting and transplanting, a cheap and serviceable one for quick jobs)
- Hand cultivators: 2, cheap (for weeding)
- Weeding knife: pointed, sturdy (for stubborn weeds)
- Hand pruner, also called secateurs: purchase good quality and fit to your hand size (for ordinary pruning); save old pruners for cutting plastic pots and wire and other blade-destroying activities
- Ratchet hand pruner: cheap, replaceable (for cutting thicker wood)
- Scissors: 2 pairs, inexpensive, lightweight Fiskars type (for deadheading and snipping delicate plants like lettuces and poppies)

ELECTRIC AND GAS-POWERED TOOLS

Lawn mowers, weed whack-ers, and hedge trimmers are helpful, unless you plan to hire people to do these jobs. I keep a really old gas-powered lawn mower for touch-ups and for making new beds.

STAND-UP TOOLS

- Shovel: good quality, pointy end, straight wooden handle, try out for length (for digging holes)
- Spade: good quality, flat end, wooden handle with D grip, try out for length (for edging and turf removal)
- Garden fork: good quality, metal, wooden handle, very strong, unbendable tines (bed preparation and compost pile work)

- Garden rake: inexpensive, short fixed metal tines, wooden handle (smoothing and preparing beds)
- Leaf rake: cheap, metal or plastic, wiggly tines (debris and autumn cleanup)
- Cultivator: inexpensive, straight line best, metal with straight wooden handle (for big weeding jobs between plants)

OTHER NECESSITIES

- Hoses, watering cans, sprinklers, nozzles, and cut-off valves *(as outlined in "Water Wisely," page 57)*
- Garden gloves: 3 pairs, inexpensive, but must fit well: one pair leather gauntlets for working with thorns; one pair rubber-tipped for wet, cold days; one regular for protection
- Stakes and white string: short wooden stakes sharpened on one end (for pounding into ground) and roll of white string (for plotting new beds and paths)
- Green twine: ball, biodegradable (for tying up plants; can be composted at cleanup time)
- Wooden plant markers and indelible-ink pen (for marking plant and bulb locations and identifying newly planted seeds)
- Muck buckets: at least 3, cheap, big plastic buckets with handles, can be dragged (for weeding and pruning, for planting, for making compost teas)
- Tall stakes: cheap, 6 feet tall, wooden or bamboo, purchase by bundle, can be broken or cut to size (for tying up plants)
- Garden cart: big purchase; good quality, wooden-sided, big wheels, removable end for dumping (saves back and legs when doing big jobs)
- Small plastic tarp: inexpensive (for weeding, collecting leaves)
- Woven weed barrier cloth: 1 roll at least; good quality, black, woven from plastic strips, reusable *(See page 15 for making new beds and paths, putting under new patios.)*

Hand Tools

Trowels

cultivator

knife

pruner

Ratchet

2 pair scissors

Stand Up Tools

2 shovels

fork

leaf Rake

garden Rake

cultivato

Other Necessities

hoses

Nozzles

connectors + valves

watering cans

gloves - 3 pair

twine

short stakes

indelible markers

cat

green   white

wooden plant markers

tall stakes

weed Barrier

tarp

Floating Row Cover

Muck Buckets

garden cart

- Floating row cover: inexpensive; white lightweight material, such as Reemay (for protecting newly planted seeds, for frost protection, to shade new transplants)

HOW TO ORGANIZE TOOLS

PURCHASE PRIOR TO INSTALLATION

- Shelf unit: cheap, sturdy, plastic, at least 3 feet wide, deep shelves (Rubbermaid makes these.)
- Hooks: large size for hanging stand-up tools
- Baskets: 3 inexpensive sturdy wicker, with strong handles
- Mailbox: inexpensive, old-fashioned type mountable on post
- Hose hangers

TOOLS

- Hammer
- Screwdriver
- Recycled wooden clementine crates or other stackable containers for organizing shelves

INSTALLATION

1. Assemble shelf unit and place in dry location (garage, basement, back porch, etc.). Use clementine crates or other stackable containers for organizing small items like gloves, markers, etc.
2. Place one of each hand tool in one wicker basket. This is your "go basket" to grab when doing ordinary chores. Store near the shelf unit.
3. Keep two wicker baskets empty but store near the shelf unit. One can be used to cart extra things like markers and gloves as needed for the job at hand. The other empty basket is always available for harvesting.
4. Mount hooks for hanging stand-up tools.
5. When moving tools to work area, place the hand-tool basket, stand-

up tools, muck bucket, and small tarp in garden cart. Move cart to work area, spread tarp on ground, and unload all tools onto tarp. As work proceeds and you finish (even momentarily) using a certain tool, replace it on the tarp. This leaves the cart free for debris and prevents tools from being lost in borders and under plants.

6. Also, to create a small outpost where extra tools can be left, mount the mailbox to a post anywhere in the "busy" area of the garden. (For me, this is the potager.) Store extra hand tools in the mailbox (cheap trowel, cultivator, extra gloves, scissors, twine, tomato ties) to keep these items dry and accessible for quick jobs.

7. Garden cart can be stored outside. Place on end so that rain drains out. If stored near the car parking spot, the cart can also be used to bring groceries to the front door.

8. Store muck buckets outside upside-down during warm weather. I keep one near the potager next to the tool-storage mailbox. In winter, bring these inside, as they will break if repeatedly frozen.

9. In winter, use hose hangers for winter storage of garden hoses. Place all drained watering accessories in one empty muck bucket.

10. You can oil and sharpen your tools as you prefer. I'll admit that I don't do much to my tools except wipe them off if I'm not too tired. When my pruners get rusty, I oil them with a drop of olive oil, which I always have on hand.

FOUR

Record Your Progress

WHAT'S THE PAYOFF?

This small project helps you to establish a way to keep garden records. Once you have more than five plants, you need a place to write down their names. You'll also want to remember the name of that blue clematis you saw at the botanic garden, to record how many days it took the peas to germinate, and to sketch out an idea that you

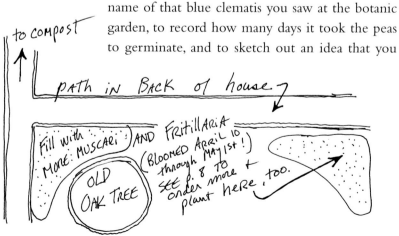

to compost

path in Back of house

Fill with MoRe MuSCARi AND FRitillARiA
(BLoomed ApRil 10
through MAy 1st!)
See p. 8 To
oRder more +
plant heRe, too.

OLD
OAk TREE

have for next summer's containers. You'll need to draw in a rough map of the new perennial bed, and to write down where you planted those wonderful tulips. A great garden happens over many years, and this is how you'll remember it all.

Artistic gardeners may enjoy keeping handmade journals with lovely sketches and paintings. Geekish gardeners may find it fun to keep records on laptops. Personally, I have kept a series of plain black sketch-books as garden journals and I work with them in a rather haphazard manner. I find most official garden journals unappealing because the format demands that you record certain things in certain ways on certain days. Although the more fastidious would definitely argue otherwise, it seems to me that it's not important how a journal is kept, but just that one actually exists *somewhere* and is written in *sometimes.*

Every gardener needs to discover an open, blank slate of choice and fill in garden information and records whenever the mood or necessity strikes. In my own journal, some pages contain very rudimentary drawings, while others just have lists of garden chores to fulfill during the next dry weekend. I paste catalog plant descriptions next to the plastic tags that arrived with the plant. (Plastic tags should never be in the garden. They and their valuable info get lost. Make a wooden marker for

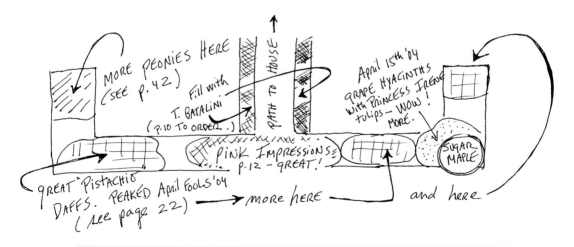

the garden and keep nursery tags for your records.) My pages are also filled with photographs (to remind me where the scillas are planted), copies of order forms (on the off chance that a refund is needed), and actual seed packets (another great source of growing information).

To organize my records a bit, I date the entries at the top of the page. Even if I can't remember the exact date something happened, just writing "Winter 2004" works fine. If you decide to keep a journal as I do, you might also want to add numbers to the bottom of the pages to make cross-referencing possible. Seeds and plants are ordered months in advance, so it becomes helpful at bloom time or at harvest time to be able to refer back to the plant's original entry: "September 23: Terrible potato yield. See page 57 and don't buy from those people again." Or, "April 2: Really early arugula. Delicious. See page 62 for packet. Buy again!"

Photographs are a vital and sometimes amusing part of good record-keeping for your garden. You can shoot a close-up of one little yellow iris next to chartreuse euphorbia sprouts to remind yourself of that cheerful combo. Or, take five side-by-side shots that can be taped together to show the entire expanse of your mixed border. Take pictures of your wintry vignettes, your son's incredibly productive pumpkin vine (my son's was named "Gourdzilla"), and take pictures of the gaping holes in your late-summer beds. The last shot will remind you where to plant dahlias next year.

As someone who never felt the urge to keep a diary, the idea of

maintaining a garden journal seemed a bit odd at first. But now I know I'll never have to worry when I forget the name of something, because that information is in there somewhere.

Years from now, your journal will remind you of all the crazy things you've done in your garden and it will inspire you to attempt all the crazy things you haven't tried yet. Expensive trowels will eventually rust or get lost, but an ongoing garden record is the trustiest tool you can own.

PURCHASE PRIOR TO INSTALLATION

- Plastic magazine files
- Small Post-it notes
- Small file box
  or Plastic shoe box with lid
- Tape
- Scissors
- Pencils and pens
- Large, plain-page artist's sketchbook
  or Other blank book
  or Computer program for garden files
  or Whatever record-keeping device you prefer

TOOLS

- Wooden plant markers and indelible-ink pen
- Clothes pegs
- Camera

INSTALLATION

1. Save all plant catalogs that you like or those from which you make purchases. Place Post-it notes on pertinent pages. Keep in magazine files.
2. When planting seeds: Mark planting space in garden with wooden plant markers. Keep seed packets for one day's sowing clipped

together with a clothes peg. Write the sowing date on the top packet. Keep pegged together and store in a file box.

3. Map out a sowing scheme. Either draw directly in the journal or sketch on paper to be taped into the journal later. Write the date on the sketch.

4. When transplanting from nursery containers: Use wooden plant markers in the garden. Keep nursery tags for records. Use a clothes peg to clip all plastic nursery tags from one planting day together. Clip pertinent sales receipt with the tags. Store in the file box.

5. Map out planting areas as per step 3.

6. When planting bulbs: Use same techniques outlined above. Most bulbs come in net bags. Use scissors to cut tag away from the net and save all tags for records.

7. When you have time: Empty file box of pegged tags onto a table. Sort the bunches into chronological order.

8. If using a sketchbook: Cut seed packets open so that both sides are readable. Tape into the book. Date the top of the page. Number the bottom of the pages sequentially.

9. Either tape in sowing map or refer to page where map is to be found.

10. Tape double-sided nursery tags to page along one edge of tag so they can be flipped over and both sides read. Tape sales receipt near tags.

11. Make sure that planting map is taped in next to tags or that a page reference is given.

12. Spring: Take snapshots of your spring bulbs. Tape into book. Make a note describing where you want to add more bulbs this autumn planting season.

13. Spring: Write down the names and colors of new bulbs as you see them in other places. This will remind you when bulb-ordering time comes next fall.

14. Summer: Sketch a map of this year's vegetable garden. Note times

of harvest, cross-reference the seed packets taped in earlier, and note when late vegetables were sown.

15. Summer: Take photographs of your beds, borders, and containers for reference.

16. Summer: Take a small notebook when making visits to other gardens. Jot down path ideas, the names of roses, sources for willow fencing, or whatever seems interesting. Transfer notes or tape the pages into your journal.

17. Fall: After you plant each section of bulbs, take photographs. Tape these near the bulb information or cross-reference the page. This will help you remember how far over the tulips go.

18. Save all old plant catalogs until you are positive you don't need them anymore.

19. Winter: This is the most likely time to work on your records. If all catalogs have been saved, cut out descriptions of plants you have ordered and tape these in.

20. Winter: Sketch in the proposed plan for the coming year's potager. Look through the catalogs you have saved and order seeds now.

Add those poppies
sow seeds mid-MARCH
SEE P. 22

FIVE

FERTILIZE EFFECTIVELY

WHAT'S THE PAYOFF?

This small project shows you how to improve the fertility of your soil so that your plants are healthy, beautiful, productive, and resistant to pests and diseases. Just as it is much more efficient to nourish your body with good nutrition than it is to rub creams on your skin, it is much better to nourish your soil than it is to try to feed your plants. This project shows you how to establish a simple routine to boost and maintain your soil's overall health and how to prepare a few special seasonal garden banquets.

The first and foremost way that smart gardeners feed their soil is with their own homemade compost, the most valuable and the easiest fertilizer to use. *(See "Create a Compost Pile," page 20.)* Compost literally puts life in your soil with humus, which is decomposed animal and vegetable matter. Without humus your soil is either pure sand or pure clay and very unlikely to support vigorous plant growth. Additionally, compost contains easily absorbed plant food and important trace elements in a safe and convenient form. Compost can be added to your soil at any time.

Compost will never burn or overstimulate your plants, and it encourages and nurtures microbial action and earthworm activity, which also improve soil health. And if that's not all, compost is free. What could be smarter than to recycle rubbish into black gold?

In addition to the balanced fertilizer in compost, you may add other organic material to your soil as needed. Nitrogen is abundant in manure and blood meal (beneficial for leafy plants like lettuce, kale, spinach, asparagus, and the lawn); phosphorus comes from bone meal and phosphate rock (add to root crops like carrots, beets, onions); and potassium is found in hardwood ash (great for flowers and fruit, including tomatoes, squash, and other vegetables).

You will find other valuable materials to feed your soil in unexpected and inexpensive sources. Wash the salt off oyster shells, crab shells, and shrimp peels. Dry the shells in the sun, place in sturdy black plastic contractor bags, and crush by driving your car over them. Scatter this around tomato plants. Collect kelp off the beach (this is the long, brown rubbery seaweed). Wash the salt off, dry, and smash it up with a hammer. This is great for flower beds. Freshwater pond scum is great, too, and does not have to be washed, dried, or crushed, just smooshed around plants.

Lawn clippings add nitrogen back to the lawn or work as nutritious mulch between rows of lettuces. Blackstrap molasses is very good for your soil, as it feeds good bugs and encourages helpful microbial action. Lime boosts soil fertility in vegetable gardens. A dose of Epsom salts is a quick way to add valuable magnesium to the soil. Finally, never mourn the snow that falls on the spring peas you have just planted. Snow is "poor man's fertilizer," bringing oxygen and nitrogen to the earth as it passes through the atmosphere.

Read on to see how to establish a fertility pantry and to establish a rudimentary routine for keeping your soil happy and healthy. I advocate gentle, natural fertilizers, but it is never wise to overdo anything in the

WHAT THE HECK IS NPK?

Serious hardcore gardeners hitch up their pants and frown over NPK all the time, but this kind of talk can very quickly take all the joy out of gardening for novices.

NPK are the elemental symbols for nitrogen, phosphorus, and potassium, the three most important ingredients contributing to soil fertility. (Here's my trick for trying to keep NPK straight: think NitPicK. Also, the words nitrogen, phosphorus, and potassium are in alphabetical order.)

In a very condensed basic lesson, plants need nitrogen for good leaves, they need phosphorus for good roots, and they need potassium for good flowers and fruits. Honestly, you can fret yourself into a gibbering mess over this. I hardly ever think about NPK; I just keep to the routine described here and everything seems happy and healthy as can be.

garden. A good rule of thumb is to avoid adding fertilizer to dry plants and avoid fertilizer applications during heat waves. Drought and heat stress plants, so you need to let them hunker down and get through the bad times without asking them to do too much production work. Take it easy and your plants will love you.

PURCHASE PRIOR TO INSTALLATION

- Manure: the older, the better. Don't put fresh manure on the garden, as it burns plants. Aged manure has no odor. Arrange with a farmer, a landscaper, or a garden center to have manure delivered in winter when the ground is frozen.
- Lime: Compute needs by your garden's square footage and follow recommended distribution on bag.
- Epsom salts: 3 big boxes
- Blackstrap molasses: 2 jars
- Liquid seaweed: 1 bottle
- Super phosphate: 1 bag or more as per recommended coverage for your square footage
- Fish emulsion: 1 bottle (This magic elixir does have a "perfume" like an old tuna fish sandwich. The aroma dissipates after a bit, but consider alternatives if you are too grossed out. I kind of like it.)
- Comfrey plants: 3 large enough to transplant into beds
- Trash can: metal, lidded, to collect cold wood ash

TOOLS

- Shovel
- Old mixing bowl: plastic preferred
- Old cooking spoon
- Old colander
- Watering can: plastic 2-gallon size is ideal

INSTALLATION

1. Winter: This is the time to spread aged manure on the garden. Transfer from the pile delivered into manageable garden cart loads. Use a shovel to fling and spread sparsely across all beds except where peonies or herbs grow. (Peonies hate manure and herbs taste better when grown in "lean" soil.) It is fine to spread manure on top of snowy beds.

2. Winter: Collect cold ashes from your fireplace and keep in a metal trash can for later use. Use only ashes from wood, not ashes from artificial logs or coal. (Note: Use caution when collecting ashes. They may hide dangerous sparks for long periods of time. Cans of hot ashes can ignite and cause serious damage.)

3. Early spring: Use the old colander to sprinkle wood ash where manure was spread earlier.

4. Early spring: Use the old colander to apply lime to the vegetable garden. Apply at recommended rate on package.

5. Early spring: Use the old colander to apply super phosphate to the vegetable garden. Apply at recommended rate on package.

6. Early spring: Spread a handful of dry Epsom salts around the base of every rose.

7. Early spring: After a rain or watering, apply a special banquet to the soil of your asparagus bed: In a 2-gallon watering can, dissolve 1 pound sugar and ¼ cup yeast in warm water filled to the top of the watering can. Mix and sprinkle on the soil where your asparagus is planted. *(See "Aspire to Asparagus," page 253.)*

8. Early spring: After rain or watering, apply a special banquet to the soil of your flower beds: In a 2-gallon watering can, use warm water to dissolve liquid seaweed as per instructions on bottle. Add 2 dollops of blackstrap molasses. Sprinkle on the beds.

9. Early summer: When tomatoes begin blooming, dissolve ¼ cup Epsom salts in a 2-gallon watering can. After watering or rain, use watering can to add the mixture to the soil around tomato plants.

10. Midsummer: For vegetables and flowers, add this banquet to soil: Fill a 10-gallon trash can and add 1-quart container of compost or old manure. Leave for 1 week in a warm spot. In a 2-gallon watering can, dilute the full-strength mixture until pale brown. Apply to vegetable and flower beds.

11. All summer: As comfrey plants establish and become large and floppy, cut back and save the large, furry leaves. Add three handfuls of leaves to a muck bucket half-filled with water. Add 1 jar of black-

strap molasses. Stir and let sit for 10 days. Ladle into the watering can and sprinkle around vegetables and flowers.

12. All growing season: Warm weather speeds the composting process. As your compost is ready, spread it all over beds where flowers and vegetables grow. (Avoid applying to herb and peony beds, as herbs like lean soil, and peony knobs do not like to be covered.)

13. Late summer and autumn: Avoid all fertilizing routines during this period. This is the time when growth needs to harden off in preparation for colder weather.

14. Late summer and autumn: Arrange for next winter's delivery of old manure.

SIX

Stay On Top Of Weeds

WHAT'S THE PAYOFF?

This small project outlines a defensive and offensive plan to prevent weeds from getting the upper hand in your garden. A quick way to make any garden area look much better, weeding is an essential part of good garden hygiene. As an added bonus, active weeding (as opposed to merely complaining about weeding) counts as exercise. According to Barbara Pleasant, author of *The Gardener's Weed Book*, weeding burns as many calories as moderate bicycling or water aerobics.

Most people recognize the names of a few villainous weeds like crabgrass, dodder, pigweed, dandelion, plantain, and bindweed. However, sometimes a desirable plant in one place becomes a weed someplace else. Mesquite, kudzu, bittersweet, and water hyacinth are snakes that were once invited in to sit by the fire. Other plants that have very bad reputations in some locales are honeysuckle, Jerusalem artichoke, morning glory, daisies, purple loosestrife, violets, and yarrow. Some people tolerate purslane, milkweed, and dandelion, as they are wild edibles, while others are not so tender-hearted. I grow Queen Anne's lace in my borders, but I have heard others exclaim that this weed has no place in a garden. For the self-confident gardener, as long as one plant does not interfere with the growth of another and as long as you like the way that plant looks, there is no need to worry about it or rip it up.

A GREAT WEED REFERENCE

The Gardener's Weed Book *by Barbara Pleasant (Storey Communications, 1996) is a concise, well-illustrated book describing most common North American weeds and how to control each one organically. This is a terrific little book for your garden library.*

However, it must be said that any garden left completely unweeded for too long ceases to be a garden. It becomes an unkempt and unproductive hayfield. If you want to maintain a semblance of garden-tude about your landscape, you should keep everything a manageable size and incorporate regular weeding practices. Maintaining a relatively tidy garden will also help to keep your waistline trim and bring you inner peace, so how's that for payoff?

I bet you can guess that I do not use chemical herbicides except in tiny amounts to deal with persistent poison ivy. *(See "Poisonous Ivy," page 49.)* It worries me that the verdict is still out regarding herbicide contamination and pets, wells, and children. I know that many gardeners use herbicides and feel perfectly safe doing so. Do what you feel works best for your household.

However, if you are interested in a safe, natural herbicide, try this relatively new discovery: corn gluten meal. Researchers deep in the Corn Belt at the University of Iowa have discovered that the residue left after grinding cornmeal contains a natural herbicide. Corn gluten meal prevents seed germination for months but is not harmful to plants that are already established. It can be used on existing lawns and flower beds with no danger at all, and it is especially handy for dealing with the pesky weeds that somehow sprout up in walkways and patios.

The easiest way to prevent a weed problem in ornamental beds and borders is to plant flowers and shrubs very closely. If you leave too much space between perennials and annuals, that space is just going to fill up

with weeds. My borders are so packed with flowers that I rarely have to weed once everything gets going. I would much rather have lush beds that shadow out weeds than stingy beds dotted here and there with flowers.

Also, I know that some books advocate the use of mulch in flower beds to keep the weeds down, but I don't like this look. If I may be blunt, it hints of gas station landscaping. Mulch also prevents annuals from gracefully self-seeding and perennials from gently spreading so that you never lose that "brand-new garden" stiffness. What could be easier or more desirable than to plant out weeds and enjoy all the extra flowers?

Unlike flower borders, a vegetable potager starts up from bare soil every year and, thus, has more empty ground for weeds to invade. Additionally, you must maintain spaces between vegetables to keep them productive; therefore, planting out weeds won't work here. When you see a lush potager packed with produce ready for picking, you can bet that when the seedlings were tiny, they were properly spaced and kept weed-free. For example, carrot seedlings are as small as threads, but if they are crowded too closely together, they will never become big carrots. As the tiny seeds sprout, check the seed packet for recommended spacing and thin the rows of seedlings accordingly. (These thinnings make delicious additions to salads.) Additionally, keep the space between rows free of weeds that will also compromise growth. Later, as the carrots' fluffy tops fill out, these bigger plants will shade out sprouting weeds and your job will become much smaller.

The first and best way to prevent weed problems in the potager is to avoid spring rototilling at all costs. *(See "Make a New Bed," page 15.)* Rototilling is essentially dividing five hundred weeds into one thousand sprouting pieces. At the end of every growing season, you should remove all the vegetable debris, lay down manure and compost, and cover everything with weed barrier cloth. In spring, remove the weed barrier and your garden is completely weed free and ready to plant.

If your potager has small raised beds, the paths should be kept completely weed free with a permanent covering of woven weed barrier cloth disguised with lovely mulch. (This is described in detail in "Pick Your Own Salad," page 209.) Inside the raised beds, mark the rows where you plant seeds and leave at least enough room to scrape your hand cultivator in between the rows. Transplanting vegetable seedlings from nursery six-packs also makes discerning weeds an easier task. If you cultivate your potager on a sunny dry day, you can leave the weedlets right on top of the soil to wither harmlessly away.

Preventing a weedy lawn is more a matter of attitude than anything else. A monoculture of one certain grass is not a realistic ecosystem. A modern gardener should never aim for that 1950s dad–type lawn that was supposed to look like a putting green. Honestly, that look involved all work and no play. It's far less stressful to turn away from a few dandelions and clumps of onion grass or crabgrass than it is to fret over them. If the weeds get on your nerves, get out there and pull up enough to satisfy yourself. It is more aesthetically productive to keep the lawn

you have neatly cut and edged than it is to sweat over an inevitable polyculture of plants.

In general, garden areas fall into a seasonal routine regarding weeding. During the first month of the growing season, you should aim to weed every week. This keeps the job light and easy. Thereafter, you can probably manage with a twice-monthly cleanup. Use dry days to cultivate shallow-rooted weeds and wet days to pull up the deep-rooted ones. In between, as you stroll the garden and see a weed getting ready to make flowers, just knock its head off and keep going. Other attack plans are covered in the instructions below.

Although some people do, I never put weeds in my compost piles. Since I use the cold composting method, I can't be sure that the seeds and sprouting parts will be killed. I recommend burning weeds in the rubbish pile (*not* poison ivy; see "Poisonous Ivy," opposite) or just bagging them and sending them out with the rest of the garbage.

PURCHASE PRIOR TO (DE-)INSTALLATION
- Vinegar: 1 gallon, cheap
- Corn gluten meal: 5-pound bag, available in garden supply stores

TOOLS
- Hand cultivator
- Weed knife
- Stand-up cultivator
- Tarp
- Muck bucket
- Spray bottle

(DE-)INSTALLATION

1. Plan to weed once a week during the first month of the growing season. After that, twice monthly should keep weeds under control.

2. Weeding is a good evening chore. Scratch up surface weeds on dry evenings and pull up deeply rooted weeds on wet evenings.

3. For ornamental beds and borders: Assuming you have planted desirable plants closely, simply hand-cultivate any stray weeds. Scratch the surface with the cultivator and use the weed knife to dislodge stray dandelions and onion grass. Spread a small tarp beside the border being weeded and toss weeds onto this. Be careful not to damage roots of desirables and, if any good seedlings are accidentally dug, simply replant and spot water.

4. In ornamental beds, watch for dodder and bindweed accidentally imported from nurseries. Dodder is a parasitic plant that looks like a tangle of orange threads twisting around plant stems. Bindweed looks like low-rent morning glory and is classified as one of the world's worst weeds. Both of these renegade members of the altogether more wonderful morning glory clan must be diligently handpicked off your precious plants.

5. When one area is weeded, slide the tarp farther down the border and repeat until finished.

6. Dump weeds into a muck bucket and leave in the hot sun for about one week so that plants wither and dry out completely. Either burn them on the rubbish pile (but *not* poison ivy, see "Poisonous Ivy," at right) or throw out with garbage.

POISONOUS IVY

The title above is not a typographical error. Exposure to poison ivy, either when it is alive and growing or as it is being eradicated, has put people in the hospital with terrible reactions. Even if you are not affected by this noxious weed and can pull it up with your bare hands, be aware that anything you touch afterward—tools, doorknobs, faucets, clothes, and even the tub where you bathe—can become contaminated and inflict pain on someone who is allergic or who has a compromised immune system. Poison ivy is the one instance where an extremely judicious use of a special herbicide is condoned. Purchase special poison ivy herbicide and follow the directions exactly.

Never burn or pour boiling water on poison ivy. The smoke and steam carries the poison, which can enter the lungs and irritate the eyes.

7. In the vegetable garden, keep paths weed free with woven weed barrier cloth and mulch as described in "Pick Your Own Salad," page 209.

8. Hand-cultivate between rows of vegetables. Be careful not to disturb seedlings of desirable plants. As vegetables grow larger and are thinned to proper spacings, you may use the stand-up cultivator if desired. Dispose of weeds as per step 6.

9. To keep patios and garden paths weed free, underline with weed barrier cloth when under construction. *(See "Determine a Destination," page 81, and "Plot Some Paths," page 97.)*

10. If paths and patios are already established, there are several ways to keep weeds at bay: (a) Boil water in a teakettle and pour directly on weeds. (b) For broad-leaved weeds like dandelions and plantain, use a spray bottle and squirt a jet of undiluted vinegar to cover the leaves on a hot sunny day. Repeat daily until the weeds are dead. (c) Scratch weeds with a weed knife and sprinkle with corn gluten meal. (d) Overturn a pot on top of a stubborn weed. Place a stone over the hole so that no light reaches the weed. After 1 week, remove the pot and hand-pull the weakened growth. Dispose of weeds as per step 6.

11. If desired, spot-weed lawn with a weed knife and dispose of weeds as per step 6. This process is best executed after a period of rain. Vinegar spray will not work on lawns, as it will kill the surrounding grass along with the weeds.

SEVEN

Don't Get Bugged

WHAT'S THE PAYOFF?

This medium-sized project helps you to prepare lines of defense against bad bugs. This project also shows you how to assemble an organic arsenal should the need for offensive actions be required. Deterrence is always a first strategic choice, but should the bad bugs break through, you will be ready to strike back right away.

A smart gardener's first line of defense is built into all the projects and methods described in this book. An organic garden with a strong ecosystem has less chance of getting infested with bad bugs in the first place. Strong plants, hungry birds, and hungry good bugs all help keep the nasties at bay. Also, as the entire premise of this book is that you want to be out there in your garden doing things, you are more likely to spot bad bugs upon their earliest arrival date and make them unwelcome before they get the upper hand. The old-fashioned way to get rid of bugs used arsenic, mercury, and many other undesirable poisons. The new-fashioned way is to wander outside with your morning coffee and observe how many aphids your hummingbirds eat. *(See "Attract Birds," page 64.)*

An organic gardener has many allies to call upon in the battle against bad bugs. Wild birds, ducks, chickens, guinea fowl, toads, snakes, salamanders, centipedes, and spiders eat lots of bad bugs. Beneficial bugs, including ladybugs, praying mantises, aphid lions, fireflies, dragonflies, lacewings, and beneficial wasps, also gobble up bad bugs.

Raccoons, possums, skunks, bats, and moles also eat bugs, but tolerance for these critters has to be weighed against the damage they sometimes create. (To keep moles from flower beds, push kiddie whirly-gigs into the soil to rattle in the wind and annoy the super-sensitive moles.) Another example of watchful tolerance involves the tomato hornworm. This large, gross-looking caterpillar can eat almost an entire tomato plant but should not be killed if he sports small white egg sacs on his back. Those eggs were laid by a beneficial wasp and the hatching babies will eventually kill the hornworm and hundreds of other baddies, too.

This project does not involve a lot of purchasing, but is more about assembling a "Don't Bug Me" area near where you store your tools. Items can be organized on shelves or kept in big muck buckets. The point here is that your garden time is probably limited and you don't want to have to root around the house for supplies or run to the store. In battle, readiness is everything.

ITEMS AND TOOLS TO PURCHASE OR GATHER

- Liquid soap: bottle of Dr. Bronner's, Ivory Liquid, or Murphy's Oil
- Vegetable oil: small bottle of cheapest kind
- Squeezable squirt bottles: recycle ketchup, mustard, and shampoo containers for applying dry and wet potions

- Spray bottles: cheap, for applying wet potions
- Masking tape and indelible marker: for ID'ing contents of containers
- Scissors: cheap and sharp
- Jet nozzle for hose
- Gallon milk jugs: for storing concoctions
- Funnel
- Floating row cover
- Rain or well water: untreated and soft water mix best
- OPTIONAL: old blender
- Strainer: large, fine mesh
- Baking soda: store in plastic
- Tabasco sauce: big bottle
- Chili powder: purchase in bulk, keep dry
- OPTIONAL: gloves and safety glasses for handling chili and Tabasco sauce
- Cinnamon: purchase in bulk
- Ammonia: gallon jug
- Sticky traps: keep dry and wrapped until ready for use
- OPTIONAL: Havahart trap, woodchuck size best for most uses
- Wood ash: keep dry
- Diatomaceous earth: keep dry
- Aluminum foil: heavy-duty roll
- Basket: for storing all herb clippings

WHAT IS DIATOMACEOUS EARTH?

This gritty material is crushed ancient marine crustaceans. It is mined from the ground and is not harmful to humans or pets. When applied to beetles, grasshoppers, and other hard-shelled insects, the gritty stuff seeps into the cracks in their shells and makes the bugs dry out and die. Slugs and other soft-bodied bugs don't like to crawl across the grit.

OTHER HERBS
THAT REPEL BAD
BUGS

*Store all herb prunings in
basket in bug arsenal.*

- basil
- calendula
- catnip
- chives
- flax
- garlic
- lavender
- marigold
- mint
- rosemary
- wormwood

**INSTALLATION: STEPS 1–12 ARE DEFENSIVE.
STEPS 13–22 ARE OFFENSIVE.**

1. To keep mosquitoes at bay: Use a porch fan, as mosquitoes cannot battle the wind. Flush birdbaths, water containers, and pet bowls with cold water from hose. Goldfish eat mosquito larvae.

2. Plant borage, a pretty blue-flowering herb. This plant attracts aphid lions, good bugs that devour bad aphids. (A more complete list of deterring herbs is at left.)

3. Plant any member of the onion family near roses to keep bad bugs away from these flowers. Choose leeks, garlic, ornamental onions, walking onions—all are attractive.

4. Transplant sacrificial eggplant plants away from area where you plant potatoes. Potato beetles adore eggplant and are lured away before potatoes have time to sprout aboveground.

5. Use floating row covers to keep flea beetles and other bad bugs off food crops. Remove when flowering to allow for pollination.

6. Use aluminum foil to wrap the bottom part of squash, pumpkin, cuke, and tomato stems. This prevents borer and cutworm damage.

7. Install sticky or bait traps purchased for specific pests as per label instructions. (For example, do not hang Japanese beetle traps near roses, as the traps contain a natural come-hither scent as a lure. Hang these traps as per instructions to get results.)

8. After pruning roses, barberry, pyracantha, and other prickly plants, scatter trimmings where Ms. Kitty or Mr. Doggie scratch around to do you-know-what.

9. Trap slugs with jar lids filled with sugar dissolved in

cheap beer. Place traps near susceptible plants. Dump and replace as needed.

10. To keep root maggots from broccoli, cabbage, kale, and Brussels sprouts, sprinkle soil surrounding plants with wood ashes or diatomaceous earth. *(See "What Is Diatomaceous Earth," page 53.)*

11. For chipmunks, squirrels, rabbits, and woodchucks, dust plants and soil with chili powder. (Be careful doing this. Chili really hurts for a long time if you get it in your eyes, nose, or other tender parts. You may want to wear safety glasses and specially dedicated gloves for this.)

12. Check for buggy infestations during daily walks through your garden If you spot a problem, proceed to steps 13 and onward.

13. For aphids, spider mites, and spitbugs: Spray with a cold jet of water from hose.

14. Leaf miner: Pick and destroy affected leaves.

15. Chomping bugs, bad beetles, etc.: Hand-pick early in the cool morning when they are slow. Drop into a plastic zipper-lock bag and leave this in the hot sun to kill the contents. Contents of bag can be used for step 19 if desired.

16. Slugs: When discovered in garden, simply snip body with sharp scissors and leave for birds to eat.

17. For persistent aphids, scale, spider mites, caterpillars, asparagus beetle larvae, white flies, etc.: Make soap spray using 8 drops soap and 2 tablespoons vegetable oil in 1-gallon jug of water. Mark contents and store. Transfer to a spray bottle when needed. Spray on all surfaces on an overcast day. Reapply weekly to kill hatching bugs.

18. Soap spray can be fortified with garlic, eucalyptus

OTHER THINGS THAT BUG GARDENERS

Mildew, black spot, rust, and fungal diseases are gross in themselves, but can also be spread by bugs. Try these two sprays for battling these maladies.

Mix 2 tablespoons baking soda, 1 tablespoon liquid soap, 1 tablespoon vegetable oil, and 1 gallon water in a 2-gallon watering can. Sprinkle on roses, tomatoes, hollyhocks, bee balm, and other affected plants. Repeat weekly.

Or mix 1 part milk with 10 parts water. Spray weekly. Store in fridge between uses to prevent spoiling.

Woodchucks can wipe out a vegetable potager in one night. These "ground hogs" are so large that their burrows can gradually undermine a building's foundation. Use a Havahart trap or call an exterminator, as woodchucks reproduce at an alarming rate.

Or, if you can find the offending animal's hole, use this technique to express your unwelcome: Stuff crumpled newspapers in the hole and push down with the handle of a shovel or rake. Pour half a gallon of household ammonia into the hole. (Caution: Be very careful of fumes. Do not lean over and inhale. Be careful.) Stuff more wads of dry newspapers in the hole on top of the wetted papers and push in with the handle as before. Add another half gallon of ammonia. Cover hole with a folded plastic tarp or layer of plastic garbage bags to trap fumes in the hole. Lay boards on top. Repeat as necessary.

oil, herb clippings, Tabasco sauce, and/or cinnamon. Mix in a blender and allow to marinate for a few days. Strain with fine mesh strainer to prevent clogging spray bottle. Apply directly to bugs.

19. Make old-fashioned "bug juice" for persistent problems: Gather about three dozen bad bugs, all of one type. Place in a blender with 1 cup untreated rain or well water. Blend. Dilute with 1 cup water and decant into a container. Allow to sit several days. Strain and spray on the same type of bug. Apply weekly. This is very gross and very effective.

20. Grasshoppers: Dust with wood ash, white flour, or diatomaceous earth squeezed from plastic bottle.

21. Ants: Dust with cinnamon powder.

22. If bug infestation is very strong, alternate potions and simply be more persistent than they are. Don't give up!

EIGHT

WATER WISELY

WHAT'S THE PAYOFF?

This medium-sized project will help you set up and plan how to use water wisely in your garden. It also tells you how to use kitchen water, how to collect rainwater, and how to set up a hose and sprinkler system. Watering wisely is a hands-on activity that helps you to realize the value of the commodity you're using. In addition, it shows great garden-tude to get out there and to keep a watchful eye on how your flowers and vegetables are getting along while enjoying some water play at the same time.

I am not a proponent of automated sprinkling systems. These so-called labor-saving devices require constant maintenance, they are expensive to install, and, without supervision, they waste water. Water-conserving drip systems can work in some instances—such as where vegetable gardens are planted in tidy rows—but my garden changes from season to season and I don't like looking at all that plastic tubing.

We have all experienced driving by a house and garden with its automated sprinkler system pouring water full-blast out into the street. Once I even saw an automated sprinkler steadily gushing a full stream of water right into the open window of a car parked in the driveway. Somehow a house and garden in these circumstances always looks very odd: abandoned by people and possessed by mechanical devices gone haywire. I know people who have automated watering systems and, as far as I can tell, the expense and aggravation of a totally automatic system just ain't worth it.

It is smart to learn to water the old-fashioned way. Most people either pay for water on a meter or have a well that could go dry during drought periods. Watering bans are a fact of modern-day life and cheating on a ban makes you liable for large fines. Likewise, an overextended or dry well can turn into a huge household expense. In fact, during extended droughts, a brown lawn is a badge of honor that says, even though you love your garden, you have your priorities straight.

Here is a piece of advice that always seems to surprise people: Do not water in the evening or at night. After I stopped watering the garden in the evenings, black spot, mildew, rust, and other gross diseases were drastically cut. Very early morning is the best time to water. Try to water early enough so that you have finished before the sun gets too hot. Although you will lose a bit to the evaporation battle, you will be ahead in the war against plant disease and fungus. I get up early before work, water, and then have the evening for relaxing or doing a few light chores. I adore Daylight Savings Time!

It may also seem counterintuitive that a searing drought may, in the long run, improve your garden. A drought and water ban will teach you which plants survive with less water. My borders actually became stronger after two drought seasons because the plants that died (delphiniums) were replaced with more drought-resistant plants (larkspur). I learned which plants love where I live and which ones would rather be in misty England. *(See "Water-Wise Plants.")*

One of the best garden trends of the last twenty years is a return to water-wise gardens. Big green lawns in Phoenix are being replaced with desirable desert plants and Los Angeles is abloom with drought-loving Mediterranean gardens. A beautiful garden is like the face of a beautiful person: the less artifice, the better. "Waste not, want not" never goes out of style when it comes to irreplaceable resources.

PURCHASE PRIOR TO INSTALLATION

- Large cheap stockpot
- Cheap plastic watering cans, at least 2, as large as you can carry full of water
- Plastic rain gauge, 2
- Large ornamental rain-collecting containers, glazed terra-cotta or galvanized metal, 2 or more

  or Large plastic garbage cans for collecting rain
- Dippers, 2
- Hose A: 1 section to reach from outside faucet to nearest bed
- Hose B: 1 section to run length of first bed
- Hose C: 1 section to run from first bed to second bed
- Hose D: 1 section to run length of second bed
- Hose: repeat above as needed to cover entire garden. (Note: Purchase shortest sections possible.)

WATER-WISE PLANTS

- *verbascum*
- *sunflowers*
- *ornamental grasses*
- *daylilies*
- *established trees*
- *established shrubs*
- *coneflowers*
- *herbs*
- *annual poppies*
- *cornflowers*
- *bearded iris*
- *yarrows*
- *succulents*
- *salvias*
- *producing tomato plants*
- *larkspur*
- *blueberries*
- *clematis*
- *honeysuckle*
- *established roses*
- *lilies*
- *asters*
- *perilla*
- *ostrich fern*
- *cosmos*
- *foxgloves*

- Hose connector/turn-off valves, inexpensive, to leave on all sections
- Oscillating sprinklers, 2, inexpensive (one working, one spare; these *always* break)
- Clockwork water timer, inexpensive (preferable to electric or solar-powered)

INSTALLATION

1. Outdoor containers with potted plants require daily watering. *(See "Contain Yourself," page 153.)*

2. Save kitchen water for watering potted plants. After you have cooked pasta or steamed vegetables, drain hot water into a cheap stockpot reserved for this purpose. (Keep it on the floor next to the stockpot for collecting compost ingredients.) Let the water cool and

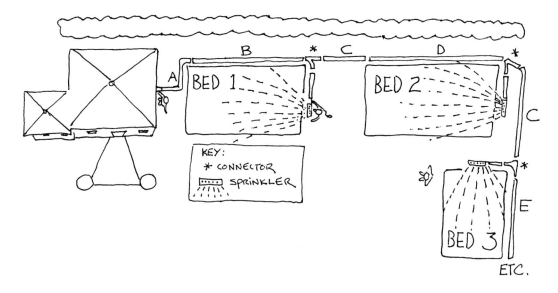

use the next morning for watering plants in pots. For efficiency, pour water from stockpot into watering can or use a dipper. This prevents uncontrolled floods of water that expose plant roots.

3. Also: Collect rainwater. Position large ornamental pots (or trash cans) so that rain falls in freely. Consider removing downspouts to allow water from your roof to cascade into rain-collecting pots. Place rain collectors under the edge of any roof—garage, shed, or carport—where water from rains runs away and is wasted.

4. Keep dipper hung on each water container. Use to carefully water containers and thirsty seedlings and to spot-water any vulnerable transplants.

5. Fill plastic watering cans from rain collectors. After use, refill and store full. This allows extra rain-collecting capacity in containers.

6. Also: Lay out a semi-permanent hose and sprinkler system for your garden. (Vegetable gardens and flower gardens produce at optimum level with 1 inch of water per week. This is almost impossible to achieve with a watering can.)

7. Self-ration your hose and sprinkler watering with rain gauges. Place one rain gauge in the vegetable garden and one in the flower border.

8. To arrange hoses for watering the garden at large (i.e., all beds, borders, and vegetable areas), attach Hose A to outside faucet. Make sure this hose is long enough to reach first bed.

9. Place hose connector/turn-off valve on free end.

10. Coil Hose A on faucet until needed.

11. Place Hose B along the length of the first bed. Hide this hose at the back or behind tall plants. Leave Hose B stretched out in place.

12. Place hose connector/turn-off valve at far end of Hose B.

13. Run Hose C from the first bed to the second bed. Attach the connector/turn-off valve at the far end. Coil connecting Hose C and conceal until needed.

14. Place Hose D along the length of second bed. Hide this hose at the back of the bed or behind tall plants. Leave Hose D stretched out in place.

15. Repeat laying out bed hoses and connection hoses until the entire garden has access to the faucet water source. If your garden is large, you may need to strategize and lay out a zone system. In this instance, purchase an inexpensive multi-outlet gadget to attach to the faucet. *(See "Storage," opposite.)*

16. To water first bed: Check position of rain gauge so that sprinkled water will be collected.

17. Uncoil Hose A from outside faucet to reach Hose B laid out in first bed. Attach the hoses together with connector valve.

18. Attach the sprinkler to the far end of the hose. Turn on water and position the sprinkler so water falls into the bed. You will get wet.

19. Watch water to make sure the position of the sprinkler is correct. Wind, trees, and hedges will affect where water actually lands. Position of the sprinklers may change throughout the summer, as plants grow taller.

20. If extra height is required, place the sprinkler on a picnic bench or

small table and weigh it down with a brick or stone.

21. Watch the rain gauge in the bed to see when 1 inch of water is collected. If it has rained ½ inch during the week (even if in brief spurts), add only enough water to make the inch. Empty gauge only once a week.

22. To use the clockwork timer: The first time note how long it takes your sprinkler to create 1 inch of water in the empty gauge. Thereafter, set timer accordingly. If only ½ inch of extra water is needed, set timer appropriately.

23. To water the second bed, remove the sprinkler from its first position on Hose B. Uncoil connector Hose C. Attach one end to Hose B where sprinkler was just removed and one end to Hose D, laid out in the second bed. The second bed is now connected in a long line to the faucet.

24. Reattach sprinkler to the far end of Hose D and repeat as above.

25. If your garden is large, create water zones. Water each zone on different days (Monday, zone one; Tuesday; zone two, etc.). If it rains, check gauge and adjust accordingly.

26. Water the garden early in the morning before coffee. Attach hoses, set sprinkler, and then go fetch your morning cuppa. Go back outside and putter. Watch your homemade water rainbows, enjoy the butterflies and birds, and take pleasure in your handiwork. "Waste not, want not" never got anyone into trouble.

STORAGE

This hose layout only has to be done once in the spring and then undone before freezing weather. Hoses and all connectors should be marked and stored in the basement or the garage in winter. Drain and keep all watering cans, rain-collection containers, rain gauges, and sprinklers dry and free from freezing.

NINE

ATTRACT BIRDS

WHAT'S THE PAYOFF?

This small project outlines ways to attract wild birds to your garden with water, shelter, and food. Birds are nature's own bug zappers and are part and parcel of a well-balanced, organic environment. They are amusing to watch, too. Any gardener is wise to roll out the equivalent of an avian welcome mat to these feathered friends.

You don't need to know the difference between a cardinal and a crow to enjoy watching birds cavorting in your garden. Invite them in and soon your goldfinches will chatter and court, your doves will strut and coo, and your mockingbird may learn to imitate your cell phone ring. The familiar "yardbirds" like finches, robins, swallows, and chickadees are easy to attract and, once the bird-word gets out about your hospitality, you may find yourself regularly dashing for the Audubon book to identify more unusual visitors. The good news is that birds, like any welcome guests, are not only great at keeping their hosts entertained, but they also help out with the chores.

Birds eat an unbelievable amount of bugs. That flock of robins hopping on the lawn is devouring caterpillars, cutworms, slugs, and grubs by the gallon. The sweet little chickadees that perch fearlessly near you may be telling you that your aphids, potato beetles, and leaf miners are absolutely delicious. And the swallows careening overhead are trying their best to consume your entire mosquito population. Birds work hard for your garden.

Being a cat lover does not exclude having birds. Most birds are wily survivors and easily elude the well-fed domestic feline. In my experience, there is an occasional distressing case of murder and mayhem, but

belling the repeat offender works. Yelling *"No, no, no!"* and banging your watering can (or whatever is closest) at the first twitching signs of stalking seems to embarrass most cats into quitting. Also, if you have ever watched a mockingbird dive-bomb a cat into summer-long submission, you'll see that nature has ways of evening up the score.

PURCHASE PRIOR TO INSTALLATION

- Bird food plants: as many as you have room to plant *(See "Bird Food Plants," opposite, for suggestions)*
- Birdbath on pedestal
- Water pots: large, wide-mouthed
- Squirrel-proof bird feeders and suet baskets (for winter)

TOOLS

- Shovel
- Trowel

INSTALLATION

1. To attract birds, water is the first essential. Within 5 minutes of positioning big water pots in our garden, swallows began dipping in. Water pots are for swooping by and need to have plenty of open flight space around them.
2. The best place for a birdbath is a spot outside a window or near a porch. These shallow water containers allow birds to stand and flutter the water around.
3. For bird safety, a birdbath should be at least 4 feet high and about 5 feet from a large shrub or a tree. This will allow the bird to make a dash for it when necessary.
4. Fill water containers up to the top. Do not fill birdbaths to the top. Flush both regularly with cold water from the hose to prevent stagnation and mosquito larvae.
5. Shelter is the second essential for attracting birds. Birdhouses are

cute garden ornaments and every bird has a preferred housing style. (Check www.audubon.org for suitable houses for your geographic area and its local bird population.) Place houses high enough (at least 6 feet above the ground) to prevent cats, raccoons, and skunks from trespassing. Nail a piece of thin metal around the post so that animals cannot climb up.

6. Plant natural shelter for birds. Grow perennial vines like wisteria, clematis, ivy, and honeysuckle. Allow vines to tangle naturally year after year rather than buzz-cutting at the end of every season.

7. Make a brush pile. This provides welcome shelter for birds. A brush pile also attracts sow bugs, earthworms, and ants that come to eat the debris and, in turn, become bird snacks.

8. Food is the third essential element for attracting birds. Add as many of the listed bird food plants to your existing beds and borders as you can squeeze in. Place bird food plants near porches and windows for ease of viewing. Plant in generous groups so that birds can find their food easily. The one exception to this bird banquet follows in step 9.

9. Big annual sunflowers are terrific bird food plants but are not good neighbors in close quarters like beds and borders. (They tower, they droop, they drop thousands of seeds.) Make your sunflower patch in a spot of its own near the pool, on the side lawn, or beyond the edge of the vegetable garden. (See "Fashion a Sunflower Folly," page 199.)

10. Feed hummingbirds naturally. These little helicopters drink nectar from flowers like monarda, fuchsia, honeysuckle, salvia, and lilies.

BIRD FOOD PLANTS

- Siberian iris
- columbine
- fuchsias
- salvias, both annual and perennial
- monarda
- annual sunflowers ('Russian Giant' and 'Giant Grey Striped')
- honeysuckle vines
- viburnum
- fruit tree (cherry, peach, medlar, apple)
- blueberry bush
- elderberry
- shadbush
- biennial verbascum
- rudbeckia
- trumpet vine
- Virginia creeper
- nandina
- holly
- ivy
- ornamental grasses
- asters
- lilies

Nectar-producing plants are far better for feeding hummingbirds than feeders filled with sugar water. Hummingbirds also eat gnats.

11. Many birds eat the berries and seeds produced after flowers are pollinated and shriveled. Curb your deadheading urges and allow fruit, berries, and seeds to develop. Leave seed heads intact until spring cleanup time.

12. Winter-feeding is necessary in areas of snow cover. It is very simple to provide a variety of feeders that dispense sunflower seeds, thistle seed, and suet cake (for the bug-eaters). Hang these from trees, from your clothesline, or anyplace you can watch from wintry windows.

13. Water for birds is important all winter. If your birdbath is not frost-proof, provide fresh water daily in unbreakable plastic or metal bowls. Each morning, bring bowls inside and run under hot water to thaw. Dump ice and refill with fresh water. (I have never used a submersible heater to keep the water from freezing, but I understand that they do work.)

use sunflower heads as natural bird feeders

TEN

WHAT'S THE PAYOFF?

This is a large project with a huge payoff. Here you will learn how to install a reliable deer fence to protect an area with a perimeter of 300 feet or less. You will also learn how to expand your deer fence coverage as needed.

Oh my goodness, the crying I've witnessed when it comes to deer leveling a garden. I cannot think of any garden complaint that has loomed larger in the last two decades. Since the 1980s, gardeners have graduated from bars of cheap soap suspended from rosebushes (which makes the garden smell like a bus station) to countless iterations of nasty sprays (all based on even worse odors) to keep deer away from their plants. The hard fact is that there is no spray noxious enough to keep deer permanently grossed out. Furthermore, there is no plant that is deer-proof. Deer will eat anything. I have even heard of deer walking up flights of deck stairs and, in one night, completely consuming a brand-new Pawleys Island hammock from stem to stern.

In my experience, the only way to protect your garden and your sanity from herds of marauding deer is a tried-and-true deer fence, at least 7 feet high and made of heavy-duty black polypropylene with 1¾-inch squares. This type of deer fencing is not like bird netting, but more like standard wire mesh—except far easier to install. The fence can be loosely stretched between trees or hung from tall fence poles.

I have seen every electrical system and fancy kangaroo barrier out there, and this is the only deer fence that consistently works for me and for others. We began with this type of fence twelve years ago to protect a large sunflower folly and have gradually expanded to enclosing the entire perimeter of our planted acre. *(See "What Kind of Deer Fence?" at left.)*

It is important to begin fencing in a small area of your garden—perhaps a favored hosta bed, a vulnera-

WHAT KIND OF DEER FENCE?

All the fencing that I use is available by mail-order or online from Benner's Gardens. Benner's fence is virtually invisible from 20 feet away, yet sturdy enough to remain intact for years of sun and freezing temperatures. One roll of fence is 330 feet long and 7 ½ feet high. The material can be cut with hand pruners.

ble vegetable potager, or your rose garden—to get the hang of putting in fence. As you get up to speed, you will see how easy it is to expand your coverage. *(See "Increase Your Coverage," page 74.)* This project explains how to enclose a salad garden that has a perimeter of 20 feet by 20 feet.

PURCHASE PRIOR TO INSTALLATION

- 1 roll deer fence (330 feet long and 7 ½ feet high; you will have leftovers.)
- 20 fence posts with cut-out "U" shapes for hanging fence *(see illustration);* 9-foot-tall posts are the best for this use. (This is enough posts for entire roll of fencing. You will have leftovers on this 20 x 20-foot example.)
- 10 bamboo poles, 8 feet long and 1 inch in diameter
- Rags, white, to be ripped into strips
- Heavy-duty treated twine

TOOLS

- Garden stakes and string for plotting
- Crowbar
- Stepladder, 7 feet tall
- Mallet or hammer for pounding in fence posts
- Safety glasses
- Old pruners for cutting fence

INSTALLATION

1. Use small garden stakes and string to plot the area you will fence. If there are trees nearby, you can use their trunks as substitute fence poles, so mark your perimeter to include them. Since this fence is remarkably unobtrusive, you need not worry about irregular boundaries.
2. Plan where the opening into your fenced-in area will be. This "doorway" should be wide enough to accommodate a garden cart.

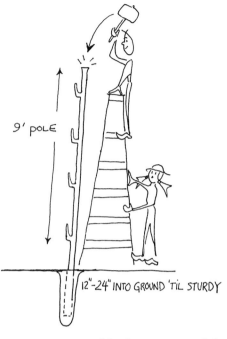

9' POLE

12"-24" INTO GROUND 'TIL STURDY

Anything less than 4 feet wide is probably going to end up annoying you.

3. Drive your first fence pole on the right-hand side of your planned doorway.

4. If your soil is rocky or extra hard, use a crowbar to start the posthole. Once there is enough room to insert the bottom of the pole (the bottom has the metal flange), you will need to use the stepladder to reach the top of the pole. It is easier on your arm if you use a mallet to pound in the fence pole, but a regular hammer will do. Try to set the post at least 1 foot into the ground, but if your soil is very sandy, it needs to be deeper.

5. Moving to your right, plot the location of your next fence post. Since this fence works best if it is not taut, you can allow up to 10 feet between supports. I use bamboo poles to prop up any extra droopiness between metal poles.

6. Once you have 2 supports, unroll enough of the fence material to hang this first section. Beginning with your first pole, leave 1 foot of fence material to the left of the post, and attach fence on cut-out "U" hooks on the post. (This extra edge left hanging will become part of the door later.) You will see that the fence simply hangs on the post. At the bottom, flare out the last few inches away from the garden.

7. Next, unroll fencing and attach to the second support, once again flaring out the bottom away from the garden. If you are using a tree as a pole substitute, run the fence around the outside of the tree. Use a small tack to attach directly to the tree or tie twine around the tree trunk and attach the fence to that with more twine.

8. Don't cut the fence. Just keep pounding in the posts, unrolling fencing, and attaching the two together. At this stage, you should be amazed at how easy this is to do. Traditional fences require professional installation, but this is a whole new ball game.

9. As you move around the enclosed area, keep hanging the fence loosely between poles. When you approach the planned opening, pound in a fence post that is at least 4 feet to the left of your first post. This post will be the left side of your doorway.

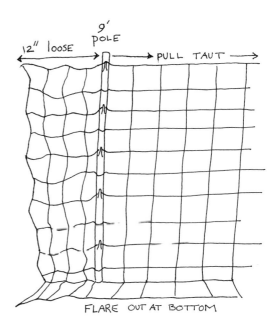

FLARE OUT AT BOTTOM

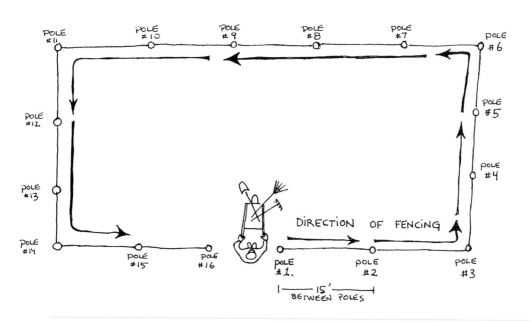

DIRECTION OF FENCING

INCREASE YOUR
COVERAGE

This is exactly how we began fencing in our property. After we saw how easy the fence was to install and how well it works, we kept linking more and more areas together. To expand your original area, move the poles farther apart and rehang the fence in longer lines. When you reach the end of your original piece, either tie on more or add a pole and keep going.

10. To make the doorway, unroll enough fencing material so that the part to the right of your final post extends far enough to overlap with the extra you left hanging from the first post. These 2 ends will be overlapped and tied with twine like a double-breasted suit jacket closed with string instead of buttons. (To open the door, simply untie your slipknots or bows and let the edges flop open. You can use clothespins to clip the doorway material back to the fence so that it doesn't get caught in the wheels of your cart.)

11. Allowing for the extra material for your door, cut the fence using a pair of old pruners or extra-heavy-duty scissors. Be very careful of the cut edges, as this plastic is as sharp as wire. I recommend wearing safety glasses when working with the edges of this fencing.

12. Adjust the fencing between supports for best coverage. Tie strips of white rags to the fence at deer-eye level to show these creatures that a fence is now here.

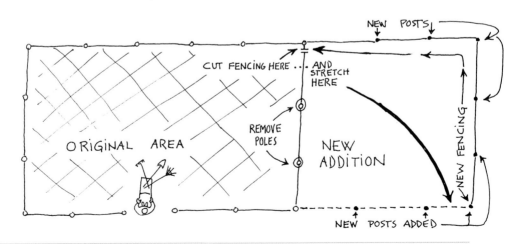

13. It is almost impossible for a deer to jump over this fence. However, they may bump into it for a while, but as it is easy to adjust and readjust, this is very unlikely to damage your work. After a while, you can remove the white rags.

FINESSE YOUR SYSTEM

Two long edges of our property now have hedges with this fencing running along the outside. This prevents those sneaky deer from squeezing in between privet stems. The hedge is trimmed with the fencing in place.

After a long winter of blowing snow and ice, you will need to adjust and rehang some of the fence. This is a very pleasant chore on a spring afternoon and, in a very small way, reconnects us with the agricultural custom of "walking the fence-line."

II.

KEEP GOING: GET OVER YOUR DESIGN DILEMMAS

You can throw all the plants in the world into your yard and still not have a garden. Design is important. The second section of *The Way We Garden Now* introduces you to the elements of doable design: destinations, walkways, rooms, and vertical elements. Good design is not scary at all if you just think about it as a way to make your garden work and look nice at the same time.

If everyone could afford to hire interior decorators, professional personal shoppers, and garden designers, then the whole world would be equipped with someone else's blueprints for almost all aspects of their everyday living. However, I am here to let you in on a Little Design Secret: Almost anyone can figure out design challenges all by themselves and, in the process, experience good, creative mojo that raises your overall confidence. I am also here to tell you the One Big Design Secret: Just do it and it will work.

Hiring a garden designer can be a wonderful way to get all your garden desires organized into one set of plans. I have many designer friends and I adore seeing what they accomplish, but I also adore figuring things out for myself. I have had the opportunity to spend twelve years in my current garden, yet there are still annoyances that need tweaking in its design. These imperfections in my garden allow me to constantly daydream about how I could make things better and, frankly, keep me excited about embarking upon the next project. As long as you don't overcommit and pour a huge concrete "surprise" in the middle of your garden, you can always rearrange your design elements to suit your expanding visions.

The first three projects describe the process of using design to lure people out into the garden.

The next two projects describe how to make the halls and walls (paths and hedges) that make your garden a living space.

The last three projects in this design section show you how to create a bit of pizzazz in your garden design using vertical elements. The notion of verticality is here divided into small, medium, and large projects, allowing you to experience this leap of design faith incrementally.

GET VERTICAL IN A SMALL, MEDIUM, OR LARGE WAY

weed → Barrier

tarp

Floating Row Cover

Muck Buckets   *garden cart*

ELEVEN

Determine A Destination

WHAT'S THE PAYOFF?

This small project shows you how to determine your garden's destination (or destinations) and how to create a sense of "there" there. Every garden, no matter how large or small, needs at least one destination. A garden without one is like an essay with no point of view: There's a lot of stuff in there, but to what purpose? The first part of the project describes how you figure out where your destination should be, and the second part describes the extremely simple way to make your destination beguiling. After completing this project, your garden will have its purpose: a nice place to sit, nap, or dine.

If you feel that your garden does not naturally beckon you to enter it except to complete tasks and accomplish chores, then you definitely need to make a change. I once visited a large garden made by a very accomplished horticulturalist. This garden had astonishing plant material, but not one place to sit down. The visit was exhausting, like going to a huge museum with great paintings but no place to rest and absorb all the beauty. A truly enthusiastic gardener enjoys vigorously working in the garden, but balances this healthy activity with restful outdoor relaxation. If one labors, it only makes sense to enjoy the fruits (and flowers) of one's labors.

To find the perfect spot to develop into a destination, look around and see where the lawn furniture has ended up. There may be two chairs in a warm spot where you like to have early-morning coffee, or a lounger in a shady place that is perfect for weekend reading, or the picnic table that was dragged out to the best cookout spot, or the cushions still resting at the perfect sunset-gazing point. All of these are potential spots to cultivate into enticing garden destinations. A garden can certainly have more than one destination, especially if you want a small spot near the house and a larger spot farther out into the garden.

For example, you may already know that the summer cocktail hour *à deux* is usually celebrated informally on lawn chairs just outside the

kitchen door. Even if this small spot is right up against the house, it can become a simple destination. With a tiny bit of thought, it can become an extension of your kitchen, a resting spot where you can get away from the heat, shuck the corn and shell the peas, and where you and someone else can relax and chat before dinner. Even the most modest destination will make a vast difference in your garden enjoyment.

There is a caveat to creating any destination: What's the view like? Do you see only your own beloved garden or is there a lot of "borrowed scenery" beyond your property line?

You may see the tops of your neighbors' trees (nice), or a fascinating skyline (nice), or the dumpsters for your townhouse complex (not nice).

If your borrowed scenery spoils the atmosphere of your destination, you should consider making adjustments. This can be as simple as moving the lawn chairs farther away from the back door and repositioning everything so that your own tidy back porch is what you see. Or maybe you adjust the position so that you look in the other direction and have your backs to those darn dumpsters. Either way, this is like moving the living room sofa and chairs to face the fireplace rather than the radiator or a blank wall. It's that simple.

If you have room in your garden, you may also want a second destination that takes you further afield into the veritable bosom of your handiwork. You may want to have one spot where the entire family can gather and another, quieter spot for napping. My garden has separate destinations for the following purposes: a small spot for two for early-morning coffee, a double chaise under a pear tree for singles or doubles resting events, another small spot for a hammock heaven, and a big central spot for outdoor dining. Each venue has its own feel and offers a unique position for garden viewing.

PURCHASE PRIOR TO INSTALLATION

- Garden chairs: 6 cheap, lightweight, comfortable chairs. If your garden is tiny, you will need only 4 or, possibly, 2. These inexpensive items can eventually be replaced by nicer pieces of furniture as your budget allows, but for now, mobility is key.

- Garden table: 2 small side tables, cheap, lightweight, big enough for resting a glass or two
- Garden lounge chair: cheap, waterproof, foldable is nice
- Garden dining table: choose a cheap and cheerful folding table to suit the number of people who would conceivably be invited to eat at your house. The table and garden chairs should work together. Make sure that the chairs are the proper height. No one enjoys eating with his or her chin on the table.

INSTALLATION

1. Take one chair and place it where you think you might want to sit and drink coffee in the morning.
2. Place one side table with the chair.
3. Go back inside until coffee time the next morning.
4. Next morning, take your coffee cup and walk directly to the proposed coffee-drinking position. Was it too far? Did you like or dislike the dew making your feet wet? Once you sit down, is the view pleasant? If yes, enjoy. If no, adjust chair placement accordingly. You may want to sit closer to a flower bed than you would expect to watch bees and birds on early-morning rounds.
5. Once you have found your coffee spot, move another chair and side table to make an invitation for quiet company.
6. To find a quiet nap destination, go outside after lunch and locate a shady spot for the lounge chair. Position it and relax for at least a half hour. Determine if the sun becomes obtrusive or if outside interferences bother you, and reposition the lounge chair accordingly.

7. To determine a dining destination, you must find a level spot large enough for your table and close enough to the house for food transportation. No one wants to walk the back forty with a plate full of sloshing hot baked beans.

8. Have enough plastic chairs for everyone who will eat at the table *and* for the morning coffee spot. It is annoying to have to move furniture around constantly.

9. If you plan to use this dining destination mainly in the evening hours, make sure to take advantage of any sunset views. Also plan for candles and hurricane lanterns for lighting. If yours is an urban garden and streetlamps or noisy neighbors overhead intrude upon the mood, consider using a large market umbrella to shield the table and create privacy.

10. Consider enhancing your dining spot by planting an area of white flowers that will glow at night. (See "white for night" information on page 177.)

11. Allow plenty of time for test-driving your garden's destinations. Once you discover that you just can't wait to get outside to sip, nap, or eat, consider making your destination permanent à la "Build a Dad-io Patio," page 86.

TWELVE

Build A Dad-io Patio

WHAT'S THE PAYOFF?

A large destination patio for dining and lounging can be a big, rewarding do-it-yourself project. Frankly, it can also be a somebody-else-did-it project. Either way, a bit of upfront design thinking will ensure that your Dad-io patio is the destination of your dreams.

My garden has two very large mixed borders that, at one time, presented me with far more work than enjoyment. Early one summer morning, I was gazing out the bedroom window at these borders and I realized that they were actually quite beautiful, but there was no reason why anyone would ever make the trek out there to see them. Immediately, I ran downstairs and grabbed my garden stakes and twine and headed out the door. When my husband woke up and looked down out of the window, he knew that a patio was in his immediate future.

After I outlined the position of the patio using the garden stakes and twine, I checked around to see if any of the borrowed scenery was unattractive. (For further discussion on borrowed scenery, see "Determine a Destination," page 81.) I realized that from this new vantage point, the silvery metal top of the propane tank showed. No problem there, I would just let the hedge "hiding" it grow a bit taller before trimming it again. I also noted that the rusty top of the wellhead was all too visible. No problem there, either. I inverted a large empty terra-cotta pot over the wellhead, placed another large glazed pot on top, plugged the hole with a cork, and filled it to the brim with water. Voilà! A water feature that could be quickly removed if well repairs were needed. These two simple adjustments meant that the proposed patio had much nicer views.

The next part of designing this Dad-io patio was to figure out how large it needed to be. To do this, I moved the outdoor dining table, the dining benches, the lounge chairs, and the large cocktail table inside the rectangle of twine outlining the perimeter of the proposed patio. The space was too squeezed, so I moved the stakes and twine farther out. When all the furniture I needed gracefully fit in, with room for people to walk around easily, then the size of the patio was correct.

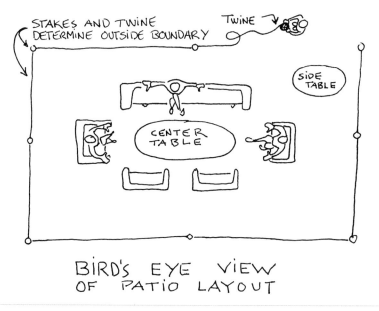

STAKES AND TWINE
DETERMINE OUTSIDE BOUNDARY

TWINE

SIDE
TABLE

CENTER
TABLE

BIRD's EYE VIEW
OF PATIO LAYOUT

The back-saving way to make a patio is to employ the method for removing turf as described in "Make a New Bed," page 15. The good news is that using this method allows you the instant gratification of having your cake and eating it, too. The weed barrier cloth that you use to smother the turf can be covered from the get-go with your choice of patio paving material. Large flat squares of flagstone or bluestone will make a relatively flat patio surface right away, while smaller material like recycled brick may result in a bumpier surface at first. This isn't a long-lasting issue, however, because if necessary, next year you can take every-thing apart and, with the grass gone, you will re-lay the patio so that the paving sits flat and the edges are flush with the ground.

A patio is a big undertaking, but once you have done one, you'll want to do another. (I have even made patios for my friends—the gung-ho process and good-looking results make this activity addictive.) A patio allows you and others to sit and relax in your garden. It also gives you a chance to admire your handiwork, gather up your garden thoughts, and consider new projects. Additionally, small patio-ettes to celebrate

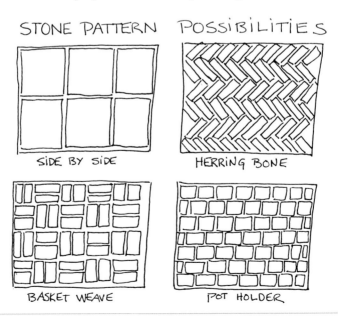

STONE PATTERN POSSIBILITIES

SIDE BY SIDE

HERRING BONE

BASKET WEAVE

POT HOLDER

seasonal delights such as the bountiful potager (page 229), your sun-flower folly (page 199), or the butterflies in your petite prairie (page 182) are a way to establish further design elements elsewhere in your garden. A well-placed patio is a natural extension of your overall garden design and delight.

PURCHASE PRIOR TO INSTALLATION

- Woven weed barrier cloth to cover the entire patio area
- Pavers to cover entire patio area. (Bluestone, concrete squares, and pre-formed amalgam pieces work best. Recycled bricks are a bit trickier but fine.) Arrange to have pavers delivered on pallets.
- Builders' sand: 3 bags or more as needed

TOOLS

- Garden stakes and twine
- Lawn mower
  or Weed whacker
- Newspapers: several big stacks
- Scissors: sharp enough to cut woven weed barrier cloth
- Broom: heavy-duty outdoor type best

INSTALLATION

1. Using the garden stakes and twine, plot the perimeter of your patio as per the design suggestions above. The patio must be on level ground.
2. Cut the grass inside the perimeter as short as possible using a lawn mower or weed whacker.
3. Use the hose to wet down the stubble of grass.
4. Cover this area with thick layers of newspapers.
5. Wet newspapers with the hose. Stomp them as flat as possible.
6. Repeat step 5 to make newspapers as flat as possible.
7. Cover newspapers with weed barrier cloth. Cut to fit.

8. Wet the weed barrier cloth with water and stomp down. Weed barrier tends to be stiff, but the weight of the pavers should resolve wrinkle issues.

9. To lay the pavers, begin in one corner and place the first and second paver side by side. Adjust to make the edges a straight line.

ROW 1
ROW 2
ROW 3
ETC

WORK IN THIS DIRECTION

10. Stand on the two pavers to see if they wobble. If yes, lift one edge and pour sand underneath to level as much as possible.

11. Adjust the two pavers so that their edges are as straight as possible. It is fine to have cracks of space between the pavers.

12. Continue with the third paver, creating a line of three. Adjust as before, adding sand underneath as necessary.

13. When the entire first row of pavers is set in place, make sure that the outer edge is as straight as possible. The interior edge may vary, as stone isn't always cut to the exact centimeter.

14. Go back to the first paver laid and begin the second course of pavers. Follow steps 10 and 11. Repeat until second course is complete.

15. Stand back and examine the lines of the patio. Are the edges parallel or perpendicular to other strong lines in the garden? An off-angle patio is fine as long as that is what you have designed. If possible, check from an upstairs window and make line adjustments now.

16. Continue making courses until the patio is complete. This may

take an entire weekend or more, depending on how large the patio will be.

17. When all pavers are laid, adjust any wayward lines.

18. Finally, dump the remaining sand in various areas, right on top of the pavers. Use the broom to sweep the sand in between the cracks and spaces between pavers. (This part is very satisfying.) The sand finishes the surface, marrying the slightly different levels of each paver to the one next to it.

19. The patio is finished for this first season and ready for its first cookout.

20. Next year, if you are satisfied with how the patio has settled into the ground, there is no need to do any further work. If winter rains have washed away sand filled in between pavers, simply repeat step 18.

21. If you desire an even flatter patio, remove all pavers and stack. Roll up the weed barrier cloth and remove all the old newspapers. The ground underneath will be completely bare.

22. Place a long 2 x 4 on its side on the bare ground. Place a builder's level on the top edge of the 2 x 4. Slightly excavate the soil until the bubble in the level indicates a flat plane. An easy way to do this is to rub the long edge of the 2 x 4 back and forth so that bumps are spread out and flattened. Repeat again and again until the entire piece of bare ground under the patio is flat. (This is easier than it sounds.)

23. Unroll the saved weed barrier and lay it flat on the ground. Re-lay pavers on top of weed barrier as per earlier instructions.

24. Re-sand the spaces between the pavers.

25. Have another barbecue.

PATIO TIPS

- ❧ *Keep patio weed free by sweeping. Seeds that fly into cracks between pavers can be swept away when tiny. Applications of corn gluten meal (see "Stay on Top of Weeds," page 44) will prevent seeds from rooting.*

- ❧ *If your patio gets hot, provide natural air-conditioning: Spray the surface with water from the hose. The evaporation cools the air.*

- ❧ *If you place potted plants on the patio, use spaced bricks to raise them above the surface. This prevents staining underneath, allows the container to drain properly, and allows the entire patio to be hosed off.*

- ❧ *Keep a big cookie tin filled with votives, matches, bug sprays, suntan lotion, and other little niceties outside on the patio. This prevents trips back and forth to the house.*

- ❧ *Consider covering your furniture cushions in Sunbrella fabric. This magical cloth is comfortable to bare skin and never has to come inside for rain. (In fact, ours stays outside for snow, too, and has lasted ten years.)*

THIRTEEN

DECORATE YOUR GARDEN

WHAT'S THE PAYOFF?

This small project is a little different from others detailed here, as it's not like me to define one surefire recipe to gain garden ornament heaven. People who decorate, adorn, and ornament their environments enliven every culture under the sun, and gardeners, by virtue of their avocations, fall into the inclined-to-embellish group. The perfect garden ornament, whether simply sublime or raffishly ridiculous, is a very personal statement put onto a beloved piece of earth. The quest for that perfect ornament can be as creative as any other aspect of gardening. This project explains how to focus upon finding your perfect garden ornament and lists suggestions for positioning it for the biggest wow factor.

As far as I am concerned, the only rule about choosing a garden ornament is that it should be pleasing to the owner. Many gardeners prefer ornaments that are in keeping with the architecture of their house or that harmonize with the style of their garden. A Williamsburg-style

CAN'T AFFORD A
FOUNTAIN?

*If you decide that your garden
needs a watery ornament
(called a "water feature" in
décor language) but a fountain is out of the question, try
buying a galvanized water
trough from a farm-supply
store. Even a big bowl of
water will reflect sun ripples
up into the ceiling of the
porch—and birds, butterflies,
and pets will enjoy lapping
from it. If you are looking for
drippy noises, try a small
solar-powered circulating
pump. Personally, I haven't
had much luck with these
things yet, but I check out
every new one that comes out
on the market. Seashells,
beach glass, and colored
stones add yet another decorative touch to a homemade
water feature. Keep mosquitoes from hatching eggs by
flushing out the wigglers with
cold hose water when you
sprinkle the garden.*

garden looks great with formal obelisks and statuary,
while a country vegetable patch might feel more
comfortable with a collection of folk-style birdhouses
or a well-dressed scarecrow.

A garden ornament—whether made of iron,
bronze, lead, tin, marble, limestone, cast stone, clay, tile,
wood, glass, or even cloth—can be either formal or
informal, just as a piece of furniture is formal or informal. A classic, life-scale statue of a stag placed in a verdant rhododendron glade helps create a dignified
"country estate" air, while a perennially silly pair
of pink flamingoes adds light-hearted levity. Simple
Japanese ornaments such as stone washing basins look
right at home in very modern gardens, while objects
decorated with putti, garlands of flowers, or goddesses
add European atmosphere.

Besides being formal, informal, modern, or
antique-y, garden ornaments can be either purely decorative or they can be more or less utilitarian. (Honestly, how many people really tell time with their
sundials?) Splashes from a fountain may be useful for
hiding street noise or air-conditioner racket and allow
an otherwise strictly decorative element an aura of
usefulness. Likewise, a great scarecrow is charming and
may keep birds out of the corn patch. And when it
comes to decorative versus functional, once a curl of
jasmine twines around the top of a fancy iron obelisk,
who cares whether the ornament is for utility or
pleasure—it's pretty and that's enough.

In this project, it's obvious that the only thing you
need to purchase prior to installation is the ornament. A search for the
perfect decorative element can begin in any of the wonderful stores or

catalogs that cater to gardeners. Also, architectural salvage yards sell old columns, metal lampposts, reclaimed stone, and railings that can be recycled for garden use. Even down-at-the-heels cast-concrete yards sometimes have sweet little statues that can be "weathered" in a bucket of mud or painted with pale faded colors. To add "patina" to concrete, bang it around a bit and paint it with thinned glue and wood ashes.

If contemporary artwork is desired, try visiting the local masonry supply yard. Buy a few flat stones and stack them artistically. Or look for one stunning stone that "speaks" to you and use it like a totemic monolith to transform a flat plane of glossy-leaved ivy.

And that brings us to the next issue in garden decorating: Once you have found your perfect ornament, where in the heck do you put it? Consider this list of possibilities and let your imagination wander freely through your own garden.

- A pale stone statue positioned in front of a dark-green hedge acts as a spot of light in the distance.
- A birdbath centered in the middle of a wide path makes the viewer pause to look around.
- A bench at the end of a path invites the visitor to stop, sit, and face in the opposite direction. This allows an entirely new vista.
- Place an unbroken row of ornamental planters around the perimeter of a patio to define the space as a room.
- A tiny frog sculpture can sit half-hidden in a bed to draw attention to a special collection. For example, low-growing scented violets might otherwise be overlooked without an eye-catching ornament.
- An upright stone plinth will accentuate the horizontal branches of a native dogwood or Japanese maple.
- Any garden object that is painted white adds a glowing presence to the garden at night. (See "white for night" information on page 177.)
- Japanese lanterns can actually be used to light garden paths. Just add candles in glass votives.

- Rustic wooden tuteurs look great in the vegetable garden, especially when draped with scarlet runner beans.
- Sculptural wind chimes hung from tree branches can be useful when outside noises are obtrusive.
- It's worthwhile purchasing handsome watering cans that can be left in plain view near thirsty plants.
- A beautiful hammock positioned in the shady distance looks as peaceful as a sail on water.

In short, my advice is just drop your inhibitions and go out there and decorate. You'll love the way the well-placed ornament calls attention to new aspects of your beloved garden. And then, when the cold months come and dormancy threatens to render the barren garden a "forgotten" space, that putti peeping out from under snow or your scarecrow standing lonely vigil will signify that the urge to ornament never really sleeps.

FOURTEEN

Plot Some Paths

WHAT'S THE PAYOFF?

his large project shows you how to plan and execute several different kinds of paths for your garden. The built path described later in the Installation section follows an easy, user-friendly "first year" and "second year" plan of action.

One of my favorite vintage Monty Python sketches involves the instruction "Walk this way" and, in this project, you will invent a "walk this way" system for your garden. A path is a design element that brings order to your garden. A path indicates "walk this way" to see the roses or to get to the patio. *(See "Determine a Destination," page 81.)* Or, if a big pot has been moved to block a path, the message is "Don't walk this way." A good, sensible path allows you to be a very subtle traffic cop, and you are, after all, the boss of your garden.

A path needs to go somewhere. This requirement will help you to bring some order among the beds, borders, and vegetable areas that you have added, or plan to add, to your property. Imagine a bird's-eye view

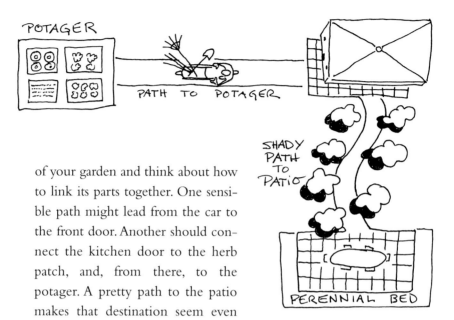

of your garden and think about how to link its parts together. One sensible path might lead from the car to the front door. Another should connect the kitchen door to the herb patch, and, from there, to the potager. A pretty path to the patio makes that destination seem even more alluring. Finally, anyplace where foot traffic has worn the grass to mud calls for a path to cure that eyesore.

Straight paths show the walker exactly where she's headed; curved paths often keep destinations a surprise. In general, straight lines tend to be more formal, while curved paths are a little more naturalistic and informal. The materials that you use to make your path can also add to its formal or informal feeling. A straight, solid, classically patterned brick path is more buttoned down than a wandering walkway of crazy paving stones interplanted with grass or creepers.

I do not recommend using poured concrete paths, as this surface eventually cracks and breaks up. My own garden path is constructed of stone set in sand and gravel. It has responded well to freezing and heat and is simple to shovel in winter and keep clean in summer.

Before moving to constructed paths, you should consider that there are different kinds of paths you can plot into your garden scheme. The virtual path is merely a visual device. When you have a line of vision

that is strongly drawn to a destination (or focal point), the pathway there may or may not actually exist. For example, when you have a bench in the distance and the way there is marked by a double lane of trees (called an allee), it is very clear that you are meant to walk down the allee to reach the bench. In lieu of an allee, a double lane of big pots or tuteurs can indicate a virtual path. If your virtual path eventually turns into a muddy mess, you know it's time to inject a little reality into the scene and build a proper walkway.

An appealing mown path through a meadow garden is simply made with a lawn mower. As the meadow begins growing in the spring, use your mower to cut a path into the new growth. You may add a circle large enough for a chair or two. Routinely cut your meadow path each time you mow the lawn. When the meadow garden reaches its peak in late summer, you will be able to stroll and sit comfortably among head-high wildflowers and grasses. A mown path will greatly enhance your meadow garden pleasures. (The only maintenance for a meadow garden is a once-yearly cutting in earliest spring before new growth starts. See "Plant a Petite Prairie," page 182.)

For the enthusiastic and energetic gardener, there is a fairly easy technique to build a simple path without the use of big equipment and landscape architects. This technique creates a semi-permanent but practical path in the first year using the "Make a New Bed" process described on page 15. This semi-permanent path can be renewed every spring or, in the second year, a permanent path may be cut into its place.

PURCHASE PRIOR TO INSTALLATION

NOTE: *All material amounts are based upon individual path width and length. See plotting and measuring steps before purchasing.*

FOR FIRST YEAR'S SEMI-PERMANENT PATH

- Woven weed barrier cloth (enough to cover entire path)
- Edgers to line both sides of path: cut stone, brick, or concrete material preferred. Metal rolled edging material is a second option. Rolled plastic edging is a distant, unattractive option.
- Mulch: shredded bark or cocoa hulls or pine needles or other attractive material as available in your geographic area (enough to cover the weed barrier, above)

FOR SECOND YEAR'S PERMANENT PATH

- Pavers (pavers are flat and can consist of stone, brick, concrete, concrete pebble dash composite or any mixture of the above that suits your taste)
- Builders' sand, at least 3 bags
- Gravel, at least 2 bags (leftover sand and gravel are useful when making up containers)

TOOLS

- Garden stakes and string (for plotting straight path)
  or 2 garden hoses (for plotting curved path)
- Lawn mower or weed whacker

- Stacks of old newspapers
- Old knife with serrated edge
- Sharp spade
- Trowel

INSTALLATION

1. To plot a straight path: Use garden stakes and string to plot out parallel straight lines. A common mistake is to make the path too narrow. Walk between the strings on your planned path to make sure the width is pleasing. Make sure your garden cart will fit on the path comfortably. If possible, check the planned pathway from an upstairs window and make design adjustments as necessary. *(See "Visual Tricks with Paths," at right.)*

2. To plot a curving path: Lay one garden hose on the ground to make a graceful curve. The hose will help you visualize wide curves. Tight curves usually are not a good idea. Use the second hose to make the curve on the matching edge of the path. Measure from hose to hose to make sure that the path width stays consistent. Make sure your garden cart fits on the path and can navigate the curves. If possible, check your plans from an upstairs window. *(See "Visual Tricks with Paths.")*

3. When you are satisfied with the layout of the path, measure the interior area as a guideline for purchasing materials. If the path is 20 feet long and 3 feet wide, you will need to purchase materials for 60 square feet.

4. Using a lawn mower or weed whacker, cut the grass in your proposed path as short as possible.

5. Water the stubble thoroughly.

VISUAL TRICKS WITH PATHS

Any straight path will seem longer if you make the far end slightly narrower than the near end. There is no hard-and-fast formula for this. Simply adjust your stakes and strings and look to see if the trick is working or if the effect is too contrived.

For a curved path, adjust the width around a bend slightly by consistently moving one hose closer to the other. Since this is a visual trick, there has to be some distance involved, but the best way to monitor the effect is by eye-balling the hoses and adjusting appropriately.

6. Lay a thick layer of newspapers on top of the wet ground.
7. Soak newspapers with water and stomp on them to flatten.
8. Cut weed barrier cloth and completely cover the newspapers.
9. Water again.
10. Line both sides of the weed barrier path with your chosen edging material. Leave tiny gaps for water to escape from the sides.
11. Spread mulch to hide the weed barrier. Edgers will keep mulch on the path and out of the lawn.
12. Water well to ensure that the path drains properly. Space edgers so that puddles can drain.
13. Walk on wet mulch to settle it into place.
14. This semi-permanent path will remain completely weed free. The path can be renewed each spring or lifted and a permanent path installed in its place.
15. Next year, the entire area under your path will be bare. You can renew mulch or install a more permanent path as described below.
16. Before cutting in a permanent path, decide if you want a solid construction of tightly adjoined pavers or a looser construction with spaces between pavers. Materials needed will not vary, but it is easier to make a path that has spaces between pavers.
17. For number of pavers required, simply multiply the length by the width to find out the area that must be covered.
18. Beginning at one end, cut in the first paver by the method below.
19. Lay the paver flat on the ground. Using the old knife, cut into the soil around the paver, making a complete outline.
20. Remove the paver and cut the shape deeper with the sharp spade.
21. Use the trowel to remove soil under the spot for the paver.
22. Place the paver back in its spot and see if it lies flat. Stand on it and see if it wobbles. Note where wobbles occur.
23. Remove the paver again. Adjust the area underneath with sand to create a firm bed. Use gravel where more support is needed.
24. Replace the paver again and repeat step 20 until paver is firmly set.

25. To mark the next spot, stand on set paver and take a small step forward. Try placing the second paver there to see if it is navigable. Adjust closer or farther as needed.

26. Repeat steps 19 through 25 to set the second paver.

27. Repeat steps 19 through 25 to end of path.

28. To increase the width of the path, start at the beginning and make a second row of pavers beside the first row. Adjust to keep lines parallel. Repeat to end.

29. When entire path is cut in, water thoroughly to settle. Adjust any wobblers with sand and gravel as above.

30. It is difficult for an amateur path builder to keep all lines perfectly straight. To remedy this, adjust spaces between stones and, if necessary, omit the occasional paver entirely. Fill this area in with creeping plants or seed with grass and your mistake will look deliberate and artistic.

YEAR 1.

5. MULCH

4. WEED BARRIER

3. LAY NEWSPAPER

1. MOW PATH

2. WATER

YEAR 2.

3. ADD SAND

2. STOMP & LEVEL

NEXT PAVER

1. LAY PAVERS

FIFTEEN

WHAT'S THE PAYOFF?

This large project explains how to plan and plant a hedge. The design process for planning your hedge is contained in the prose section below; planning is crucial to your eventual hedge happiness, so don't skip this part. Planting a hedge is very simple, and instructions for this process are included in the installation directions.

Adding a hedge is like playing architect in your garden. Whether hunkering down at 1 foot tall or towering 16 feet high, a hedge creates a living wall in your landscape. It can define a perimeter, provide privacy, divide a garden into different spaces, or all of the above. Hedges are part of a good yard's structure and are sometimes referred to as "garden bones." This simply means that hedges are part of the permanent skeleton that holds the more ephemeral parts of the garden—flowers, herbs, and plants—together.

As always, start small and, after a while, go bigger if you have enjoyed the initial results. It can be a costly disaster to invest in many hedge plants that you hate or that die. Hedges can also be installed in sections as budgeting allows. Newly installed sections will catch up to more mature sections fairly quickly.

PLANNING YOUR HEDGE

Study garden books and magazines for hedge ideas. Prepare a small file of images and information regarding the following questions:

- Do you want a clipped hedge or an unclipped hedge? Both types will need care and pruning, but a clipped hedge is more angular and an unclipped is more fluffy.
- Do you want evergreen or deciduous material?
- Do you want to make a mixed hedge or do you want all the plants to be the same?
- Do you want to prune this hedge yourself or do you need to factor in the cost of regular professional trimming?
- Are there local laws and neighborhood regulations regarding hedges?
- You should find out if there are local ordinances regarding hedges before investing any time or money.

Next, take your file to your local nursery for a preliminary fact-finding visit. You must consult with professionals there about hedge plant material that works in your locale. Here are a few sample questions:

- What hedge material is hardy here? The plants are meant to be a permanent feature, so they must be able to survive your winters. *(See "Possible Plants for Hedges," page 106.)*
- Are there localized pests and diseases that might kill or damage the hedge? Your hedge must be resistant to problems like wooly adelgid, rust, prolonged drought, or deer infestations. *(See "Install a Deer Fence," page 69.)*
- How much do various hedge plants cost per specimen? Your hedge must be affordable within your overall budget. Planting a

POSSIBLE PLANTS
FOR HEDGES

- *yew*
- *boxwood*
- *holly*
- *rugosa rose*
- *rosemary*
- *berberis*
- *forsythia*
- *arborvitae*
- *privet*
- *hemlock*
- *beech*
- *mock orange*

hedge is a fairly large investment in your garden.

Armed with the information you have gathered, you can now get into the really fun, physical part of planning where to position your hedge. Make a pretend hedge: Use two upright poles (bamboo works great) strung together horizontally with clothesline. Either get two helpers to hold the poles or stick them in the ground.

Hang floating row cover along the clothesline with clothes pegs just as you would hang a sheet out to dry. This is your imaginary hedge.

Stand back and examine the pretend hedge for location only. You might want a hedge to bisect your garden into the flower part and the vegetable part. You might need a hedge to hide your neighbor's hideous garage. You might desire a hedge so that passersby don't see you skinny-dipping in your pool. Once you have the basic hedge location, measure the distance between the poles. This is how long your hedge will be. You will need to tell the nursery you need plant material for a hedge X feet long.

Once you know you want a hedge that runs, for example, 20 feet from point A to point B, then you must decide how tall this hedge needs to be. Use your pretend hedge to determine height. Adjust the horizontal line of the clothesline up or down the poles until the proposed hedge height looks right and does the job you want it to do.

You might want a 3-foot-tall hedge that divides your lush flower beds from the tidy rows of the vegetable garden. This delineates the areas but provides a view over the top. Or you might need a hedge 5 feet tall to completely hide a propane tank from the patio view. Or you might desire a very tall hedge to prevent your neighbors from peering into your pool area.

Remember that a really tall hedge can be really hard to prune. It will

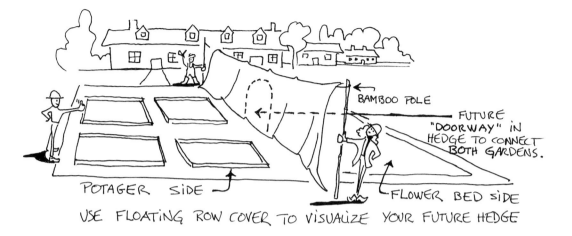

BAMBOO POLE

FUTURE "DOORWAY" IN HEDGE TO CONNECT BOTH GARDENS.

POTAGER SIDE

FLOWER BED SIDE

USE FLOATING ROW COVER TO VISUALIZE YOUR FUTURE HEDGE

also block a certain amount of sunlight. However, a hedge that will never grow tall enough to hide the silver cap of the propane tank is silly. Once you have decided the height of your potential hedge, measure from the ground up to the top so that you can tell the nursery that you need plant material that will eventually be X inches tall.

Armed with all the information you now have, make a return visit to the nursery. Purchase your hedge material and, unless you have a truck, arrange for delivery. Most nurseries will also install hedges, but having this done really jacks up the price. Often gardeners *like* the occasional big project.

PLANTING YOUR HEDGE

PURCHASE PRIOR TO INSTALLATION

- Hedge material
- Compost, handful for each hole (if you don't have your own)
- OPTIONAL: Seed packets for cosmos, cleomes, or other tall, wispy annual flowers

GROW MORE HEDGE

Most of my hedges are privet because I once read that this deciduous plant is easy to propagate. It is! When the hedge is pruned, simply grab the prunings, strip off the bottom leaves, and jab the sticks into any fertile, watered space. I poke mine into my vegetable garden. During the growing season, most of these prunings will miraculously grow roots and can be trans-planted as a baby hedge next year. Don't you just adore freebies from nature?

TOOLS

- Garden stakes and string
- Shovel
- Muck bucket

INSTALLATION

1. Use garden stakes and string to mark the line for planting the hedge.
2. If you want a thick hedge, stagger two rows of plants with the string in the middle:

3. For a thinner hedge, plant just one row of hedge material:
4. Start at the left end and dig a hole for the first plant. Dig the hole twice as big as the root ball, just as you would when planting any shrub. *(See "Slip in Some Shrubs," page 138.)* Use the muck bucket to hold soil from the hole for easier refilling.
5. Use the hose to water the hole.
6. Add a handful of compost to the hole.
7. Backfill with soil from the muck bucket so that planting depth remains exactly the same as it was in the nursery container. Planting too deeply will cause rot. Planting too shallowly will cause roots to dry out and die.
8. Remove the hedge plant from the container. Tease out the roots and spread them in the hole.
9. Water and replace the soil, tamping soil with hands and feet so that the roots can grab.
10. Make sure the plant is standing up straight. Adjust if necessary.
11. Move to the next position. Space the plants as recommended by the nursery.

12. Repeat steps 4 through 11 until all material is planted.

13. OPTIONAL: If installing in spring, sprinkle seeds of airy annuals like cleomes or cosmos on top of the planting holes. These will sprout up and be colorful during your hedge's first, scrawny season.

14. Any new shrub (your hedge is a collection of shrubs) should receive 1 inch of water per week to promote root growth. Water at ground level if possible.

15. Do not fertilize the hedge. It is not needed and may cause die-back.

16. During the first winter, mulch the base of hedge after the ground freezes to prevent heaving.

SIXTEEN

Get vertical
In a Small, Medium & Large Way

WHAT'S THE PAYOFF?

This section is divided into a small, a medium, and a large project, each one designed to bring excitement to the flat areas of your garden. These homemade vertical elements—a twig teepee, a pea trellis, and a gourd arbor—may all be added to your garden, or you may choose one or two as you like. Whether you get vertical in a small, medium, or large way, each of these projects gives you a beautiful, sculptural form that makes a stand-alone design element or a frame for vines to climb.

Patios and paths are horizontal, hedges create different horizons, but to make your garden framework pop with interest, you need at least one or two vertical elements to punctuate your landscape. Some gardeners get it right away, while others take longer to figure this out: No matter how bountifully the perennials fill in, no matter how colorfully the annuals bloom, a garden always feels lacking unless it contains what designers call "vertical interest."

You can purchase and install vertical interest in the form of beautiful wooden tuteurs, wrought-iron obelisks, elaborate trelliswork, or even an entire gazebo. All these add plenty of interest to your garden, but frankly, they cost plenty of money, too. There's no better way to celebrate a big anniversary or windfall than with presents for the garden, but in the meantime, the quickest and cheapest way to get vertical is to make simple supports for growing vines.

Any enthusiastic gardener knows that, eventually, all the room allowed for plants in any given space is going to be taken. Creating the vertical structures in this project allows you to grow even more plants, thus solving two dilemmas in one project. Vines are the answer to verdant verticality, but the vertical elements here look pretty great in their bare forms, too. (We should all be so lucky.)

Since different types of vines have different ways of climbing, the three vertical elements here offer different types of support. The graceful teepee support (a small project) is for annual twining vines like morning glories. The twig trellis (a medium-sized project) is for annual vines with tendrils like sweet peas. The gourd arbor (a large project) is a sturdy structure that supports different types of annual and perennial climbers.

There are many ways to insert vertical design elements into your existing garden. You can place a pair of verticals like punctuation marks on either side of an entrance to create the ta-da! factor that beckons irresistibly. You can position one or more in your beds and borders to pop out of those colorful, but essentially flat, planes of plants. You can employ one at the far end

CONSIDER THE CLIMBER

One of the fascinating things about vines is how they manage to get themselves off the horizontal. Morning glories climb by wrapping their entire stems like a snake around a support, gourds grab on with curly tendrils, and clematis hauls itself up by leaf petioles that work like a rock climber's arms. Ivy hangs on by aerial roots, roses produce wicked climbing hook thorns, and Virginia creeper walks up surfaces using adhesive disks like those found on the feet of wall-climbing lizards.

It is important to consider how your chosen vine climbs when hoping to upholster vertical elements. Wrappers are generally fine with whatever they can reach. Tendrils prefer strings or pea netting to cling to. Leaf petioles also need skinny handholds. Aerial roots need surfaces to cling to, climbing hooks need something to lean against, and root disks require a surface for adherence.

ANNUAL CLIMBERS

- morning glory
- sweet pea
- runner bean
- asarina
- cup-and-saucer
- lablab
- love-in-a-puff
- purple bell
- canary vine
- gourd
- Chilean glory vine moon flower

Tie here

of a path to draw the eye into the distance. You can line up a series of uprights to mark the edge of the garden or to delineate one area from another. And finally, you can make one great big upward-pointing statement that ultimately unites your garden to the sky above. However you decide to get vertical, I guarantee that, with this project, your garden pleasure is going to go up and up!

Your adventures in verticality will bring a surprising amount of design oomph into your garden. Think about all those medieval paintings with saintly fingers pointing heavenward and just follow the directions here to move onward and upward in your garden.

A SMALL VENTURE INTO VERTICALITY: THE TWIG TEEPEE

The graceful teepee construction is an instant piece of satisfaction that, once experienced, becomes positively addictive. This simple, Giacometti-like device is nothing more than 6 long twigs tied together about 9 inches down from the tips. If you can push the bottom ends into the soil, you can slightly bow out the sides for a pleasing roundness. Two teepees can be paired and joined with a horizontal piece that makes an excellent bird perch. I use teepees in my borders and beds and also in large containers. This teepee was inspired by the twig container supports I saw in the wonderful Elizabethan garden at Hatfield House in England.

PURCHASE PRIOR TO INSTALLATION

- Bundled willow twigs: 6 per teepee, as long as possible

  or Bamboo garden stakes, thin, as long as possible
- Garden twine, natural

TOOLS

- Pruners

INSTALLATION

1. Choose a location.
2. Use pruners to cut one end of each of the 6 long twigs at an angle.
3. Beginning with 3 twigs, create a frame for the teepee, pushing the sharpened ends into the soil in a triangular shape.

4. Gather the upright tips together and, using twine, tie the ends together. The teepee will look more graceful if you tie about 9 inches from the tips, if you wrap the twine nicely, and if you can slightly bow the twigs.
5. Add the 3 other sharpened twigs to the teepee in between the existing uprights. Tie together as per step 4.
6. If desired, place 2 finished teepees close enough that a horizontal twig connector can be placed from top to top.

PERENNIAL CLIMBERS

- *gloriosa lily*
- *wisteria*
- *ivy*
- *clematis*
- *honeysuckle*
- *jasmine*
- *Virginia creeper*
- *bougainvillea*
- *passion flower*
- *mandevilla rose*
- *Dutchman's pipe*

A MEDIUM-SIZED MOVE
TOWARD VERTICALITY:
THE PEA TRELLIS

This pea trellis was inspired by a rather long "rest period" between free-lance jobs. At our house, its official name is the "Unemployed Person's Pea Trellis" because the general feeling was that I had a lot of extra time on my hands that year. You can make your pea trellis as simple or as ornate as you like.

The basic frame takes little time and encloses a wispy version of a gothic window. Next, as time and patience allow, cross-hatching twigs are tied in to boost the idea of architecture. Then, when colorful vines grow up and cover the structure, your pea trellis looks like a living stained-glass window. This handcrafted trellis can be hung against a tall fence and used for sweet pea support or it can be used as a freestanding upright in the potager for scampering snow peas. (This is an excellent vertical element for uplifting the potager, but you should never grow sweet peas and edible peas together. You do not want to accidentally eat sweet pea pods.)

PURCHASE PRIOR TO INSTALLATION

- Bundled willow twigs: at least 24
  or Bamboo garden stakes, as long and thin as possible
- Wooden garden stakes: 4, sturdy, 6 feet long
- Garden twine, natural
- Pea netting: black plastic, small package

TOOLS

- Mallet
- Twine

INSTALLATION

1. Choose a location as outlined above.
2. The heavy wooden garden stakes support this trellis. Use the mallet to pound two 6-foot stakes into the ground about 5 feet apart. Pound in about 1 foot deep or until they are straight and sturdy.
3. Use twine to tie another wooden stake horizontally to each upright. (This is much easier if you have someone to hold up the bar. If alone, tie very loosely and slide up or down until crosspiece is completely horizontal.)
4. Tie the remaining garden stake about halfway up the two uprights. You should now have a rectangular "window."
5. To form the gothic element: Locate the middle of the top crosspiece. This will be the point of the arch. Tie the ends of 2 twigs to this point, with the remainder of the twigs hanging down to the bottom crosspiece.
6. Separate the twigs and tie each to the bottom crosspiece about 2 feet apart. Bow the twigs slightly before tying, as this will form a rudimentary gothic shape.

7. Support this shape by making a long + of twigs and tying this across the gothic shape to the wooden framework.

8. Fill in the space around the arch with as many crosspieces of twigs as you have time to add. Tie these with twine. Leave the inside of the arch bare to accent its shape.

9. To allow peas to climb this trellis, tie black pea netting to the bottom near the ground and run to the bottom crosspiece. Stretch taut and cut to fit. Tie again. If you have made plenty of twig crosshatches, the peas will climb on these. If not, run pea net all the way to the top crosspiece, pull taut, and cut to fit.

10. When planting peas to climb this trellis, make a double row, one on either side of the bottom piece of pea netting. This will double your harvest.

A LARGE LEAP INTO VERTICALITY: THE GOURD ARBOR

This gourd arbor is a permanent addition to the garden and sturdy enough to support a heavy load of vines. It takes about a day to build and lasts many seasons. Although I call it a gourd arbor, it actually is more of an "as many climbers as possible" opportunity. I usually combine birdhouse gourds (white, night-blooming flowers and large, pale green gourds), 'Heavenly Blue' morning glories (no further description needed), and dangling, edible, yard-long beans (hysterical-looking and good-tasting).

A series of gourd arbors marks the top of a hill flanking our perennial borders. Here, these verticals act as a see-through frame to lend an air of enclosure to the perennial garden. My arbors are a homespun interpretation of the enormous versions I saw years ago at the Vice Regal Palace in New Delhi. There they framed the view from the huge Mughal garden out into the woods beyond. Another way to position your gourd arbor is as a long tunnel that leads from back door to vegetable garden or between sections of your garden. Finally, gourd arbors

can be used to create a destination *(see "Determine a Destination," page 8),* especially when positioned side by side to shelter a bench or two chairs.

PURCHASE PRIOR TO INSTALLATION

- Lumber: 4 x 4, 6 pieces
- Long nails
- Snow fencing: at least 8 feet
  or Pre-made willow twig fencing, 1 roll
- Pea netting: black plastic, one small package

TOOLS

- Hammer
- Shovel or posthole digger
- Another person to help

INSTALLATION

1. Decide the location of your arbors. Instructions here are for a pair of slender arbors or for one deeper arbor. This construction takes 2 people.

2. These arbors are very simple goalpost shapes using 3 uncut 4 x 4 pieces of lumber.

3. Lay 3 pieces of lumber flat on the ground like a goalpost that has fallen over. Nail the crosspiece to what will be the uprights with long nails.

4. Use the shovel or posthole digger to make the holes for the uprights. The uprights should be at least 1 foot into the ground, or more if your soil is loose and sandy.

5. Two people are needed to wrestle the goalpost construction upright. Fill in holes and tamp firmly. If wiggly, start over on the holes and make them deeper.

6. Decide where the second (and third and fourth arbors) will stand in relation to the first and erect as above.]
                                                                ]
                                                                ]
                                                                ]

7. Loosely wrap the entire arbor uprights and crosspieces with pea netting and tie at regular intervals. This allows more delicate vines to climb the posts. Pea netting can be left intact for years.

8. To create one deeper arbor, place 2 goalposts parallel [ ] about 5 feet apart.

9. Unroll the snow fencing (or willow fencing) from one crosspiece to the next. You should have enough extra to hang down on either side at least 1½ feet. Secure the fencing to the structure and wrap the posts in pea netting as explained above. Allow the vines to cover the roof. Place a bench or 2 chairs inside this simple shady structure.

III.

GET GROWING:
ORGANIZE
YOUR
ORNAMENTALS

Short Stakes

Yes, finally, we arrive at the section about flowers. But I am here to tell you that you can waste a lot of your garden budget on willy-nilly pansy purchases unless you have a plan for how you want to organize your flower (in other words, ornamental) garden. In previous sections you have learned how to make and maintain your beds and how to create a pleasing overall design. This is the equivalent of building a firm house foundation, and then adding the architectural elements that make the house "work" correctly. After you have a foundation and walls, you get to the decorating part. But, just as it would be silly to buy twenty-five cute lamps for the living room and have nothing left for rugs, curtains, and couches, it is also silly to run to the plant nursery and buy the first twenty-five flowering plants you see. This part of the book teaches you to think about how you will purchase and organize a wide variety of beautiful plants in your ornamental garden.

The first four projects in this section make up the essential plant cornerstones of a beautiful garden: perennials, annuals, shrubs, and trees. These four key elements work together to give you a long-lasting show of ongoing color changes. You will also be able to create a fascinating kinetic sculpture of growing forms. Additionally, your four essential plant cornerstones will allow you to use various textures as a sophisticated method of injecting interest into your plant palette. Stated simply: Every garden needs some perennials, some annuals, some shrubs, and some trees. This section tells you how to play with these separately and in combinations.

The next five projects show you how to tackle flower challenges and how to add easy but unusual plants to your garden beds. The final four projects allow you to go a little crazy and add small feature beds to your existing garden space. By the time you finish reading through this section of projects, you will have a firm grasp of flower power and how to get it going in your garden.

The first four projects make up the elements of ornamental gardening.

These five projects add excitement and color to flower gardens.

These four projects show you how to make specialized garden areas.

SEVENTEEN

Plant Perennial Pleasures

WHAT'S THE PAYOFF?

This medium-sized project shows you how to plan and plant a garden bed full of perennials. Perennials provide depth and oomph to the flower garden. In most of North America, a mixed border—that is, a border that has herbaceous perennials, annual fillers, woody shrubs, and a tree or two—can be orchestrated to provide color, form, and texture for the entire growing season. (A herbaceous perennial, like phlox, dies back to the ground during its dormant winter period. Phlox resprouts from the ground in spring to bloom again in summer.) In general, perennial plants are a little more costly to purchase than annuals, but the initial investment pays off in returns. Perennials are the workhorses of the ornamental garden.

When you decide to make perennials a part of your garden life (and this should happen sooner rather than later), you'll need to educate yourself a tiny bit. To successfully grow perennials, you need to know your hardiness zone. (This is explained in the sidebar on page 124.)

HARDINESS ZONES

Use the USDA zone map on pages 294–295 to locate your area and your hardiness zone. I live in Zone 5, an area that generally does not have temperatures below −10°F. in the winter. Perennials rated for Zones 5, 4, 3, 2, and 1 can be expected to live through the winter in Zone 5. Because perennials, unlike annuals, must survive the winter in your garden, hardiness zones mark the lowest temperature that a plant will usually have to endure.

The higher the USDA zone, the higher the winter temperature will be. For example, Zone 9 expects winter temps to stay above 20°F. Unfortunately, this does not mean that Zone 9 gardeners can grow every perennial for Zones 1–9. Many perennials require a cold, dormant period to bloom. Californians have another hardiness reference devised especially for them by Sunset *magazine. California zones are calculated to include many more variables than just winter hardiness. Some gardeners love the challenge of coddling plants that are actually too tender for their area. To me, this is like inviting a finicky person to a dinner party—you must be prepared for disappointments.*

Once you have ascertained what your zone is, you are ready to begin selecting perennial pleasures to add to your garden.

There are four main ways to research perennials you might decide to purchase. One of the best-known education secrets among gardeners is White Flower Farm's catalog (www.whiteflowerfarm.com). This Connecticut mail-order nursery produces the Victoria's Secret catalog of the plant world. The photography and text say "come hither," all the models are in perfect shape, and the quality and the prices are a little higher. You will drool while you learn.

Garden books are another way to learn about perennials. I have about a jillion garden books and I recommend that you start your own collection ASAP. I recommend buying books in batches and cross-referencing specific plants. By all means, buy that book all about daylilies, but also purchase books that show great gardens with daylilies in them. You will need hands-on and inspirational material in equal amounts.

A third way to learn about perennials for your area is to visit your local botanic garden during its outdoor blooming season. Walk through the display gardens and notice that every plant is clearly marked for your edification. Note what you like and, if possible, ask for a source. Many public gardens now have retail nurseries tucked away near the entrance, allowing the visitor to go home with a great bunch of plant souvenirs.

Finally, as you begin down the perennial path, it is a good idea to purchase the bulk of your plants locally. This allows you to see the plant and to ask the person there for advice on the spot. If you need advice and there is no one to help you, get back in the car and go someplace else. A good relationship with your local nursery is the key to a great garden.

Before you embark on this project, please note that you must begin with a clean, turf-free garden bed. The easiest way to prepare a new bed is using the method described on page 15.

A good starter bed for perennials should measure about 8 feet long and 4 feet deep. Many gardeners make flower beds that are too narrow. A skinny bed will never appear lush. The bed described in this project will swallow lots of plants, so be careful of dreaming bigger until you have gotten some experience under your belt.

For my money, the best time to purchase and plant perennials is in the fall. Nurseries tend to put perennials on sale then, autumnal rains lessen the need for watering, and cooler temperatures stimulate root growth instead of top growth. A fall-planted perennial has a better shot at thriving and thrilling you year after year. Rainy autumn days are perfect for transplanting perennials. Transplanting on hot days or in strong sun promotes wilting.

TWENTY-ONE
BEGINNER
PERENNIALS

- yarrow
- astilbe
- baptisia
- bleeding heart
- coneflower
- pulmonaria
- ferns
- ornamental grasses
- daylilies
- hostas
- Oriental poppies
- phlox
- verbascum
- speedwell
- coreopsis
- monarda
- autumn joy
- asters
- snowdrop anemone
  'Becky' daisies
- Siberian iris

PURCHASE PRIOR TO INSTALLATION

This will take several trips if you don't have a truck or van.

- Perennials, buy in 3s (3, 6, 9, 12); a bed 4 x 8 should have about 10 different types of perennials, 30 plants in all. The plan outlined here allows room to add annuals, shrubs, and small trees. *(These are explained in the following three projects.)*
- Bagged compost, enough to spread 1 to 2 inches on top of 32 square feet, plus extra for planting holes (purchase only if you don't have your own)
- Notebook (as per "Record your Progress," page 32.)

TOOLS

- Garden rake
- Shovel
- Muck bucket
- Pruners
- Scissors
- Plant markers and indelible ink
- Hose with shut-off nozzle

INSTALLATION

1. Prepare an 8 x 4-foot bed in advance. *(See "Make a New Bed," page 15.)*
2. Use the garden rake to remove any stones from the bare bed. (Save stones for use when planting containers as per step 28.)
3. Top-dress entire bed with at least 1 inch of compost. Rake smooth.
4. To brainstorm your planting plan (which involves steps 4-15): Off to the side, cluster all potted plants, in their groups of 3, into 3 groups for tall, medium-height, and short plants. (Read each tag for height at maturity.) These 3 groups will help you decide if plants go at the rear, middle, or front of the border.
5. Begin planning at far left rear corner with the tallest plants. Arrange the three plants (still in pots) in a triangle with two plants at the

back and one at the point. Do not follow the recommended spacing guide—plan to plant closely. (Most planting maps mark swoops of plants, which is impossible to lay out. Make triangles, then soften them a bit by adjusting positions of pots to avoid straight lines.)

6. Take the next tallest plant and arrange another triangle to the right of the first. Allow space between different types of perennials.

7. Choose a perennial from the medium-height cluster and position these 3 pots in another triangle in front of the 2 rear triangles.

8. Stand back and eyeball the positions of these first 9 plants. Estimate how far apart to spread the groups of 3. Try to make space between different types of perennials, not between plants of the same type. Later you can fill the gaps between different types of perennials with annuals, shrubs, small trees, or large potted plants.

9. Position triangle of tall plants in far right corner as per step 5.

10. Position medium-height plants (in 3's always) from right edge in triangle shape.

11. Repeat medium-sized plant triangle between the one on left and the one on right.

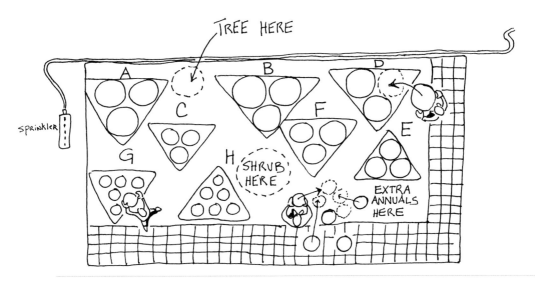

*During the first winter,
protection for newly planted
perennials is a good idea.
When the ground freezes solid
(usually late December in my
Zone 5), mulch around
plants with salt hay. The idea
is to shade the ground to
prevent alternate thawing
and freezing that pushes
perennials, especially new
ones, out of the ground.*

*Do not use pine bark
pieces or regular hay directly
on soil for mulch. The first
robs nutrients from the soil,
the second is too weedy for
flower beds. If you can't find
salt hay, evergreen branches
from your discarded
Christmas tree will work to
shade the bed. Saw branches
off the trunk and arrange in
big, overlapping layers.*

*Also, wish for snow. A
thick blanket of it is Mother
Nature's free mulch.*

12. Position 3 triangles of the shortest perennials in the front of the border. (This plan should leave one group of 3 plants still set aside.)

13. Stand back and eyeball your proposed planting plan. Move pots to avoid any straight rows. The triangles should not be rigid.

14. Adjust and readjust pots until you are pleased with the results.

15. Squash the last 3 plants in as a group according to their height. This technique allows you to be very fluid with rearranging your triangular planting guides.

16. Once you are satisfied with the arrangement of perennials, draw a map of your bed in your notebook. As you proceed with planting, remove and tape the plastic nursery tags onto pages in your notebook. These unattractive tags do not look nice in the garden and often get broken. Plus, the information on them is too useful to lose.

17. Plant the back of the border first, beginning at the rear left and moving right.

18. Unpot the first set of perennials: Water the containers deeply and allow to soak in. Turn the first container on its side and press and roll firmly on the ground to loosen the contents. Gently remove the plant from its container. Do not pull it out by the stems.

19. Examine the root ball for size. Use the shovel to dig a hole slightly wider and deeper than the root ball. Place soil in the muck bucket as you dig.

20. Place a handful of compost in the bottom of hole and water.

21. Place the perennial in hole to check planting depth. It is crucial that the planting depth in the hole remains the same as the planting depth in the pot. Planting too deeply promotes crown rot. Planting too shallowly kills roots.

22. When the hole depth is correct, prepare the unpotted perennial for planting by teasing apart the roots a bit. If they are tightly wound, carefully cut 3 slits in the sides with scissors to allow them to spread out. Tightly wound roots will continue to grow in circles if not teased out.

CUT ROOTS

23. Place the perennial in the prepared hole and fill in half of the soil needed from that set aside in muck bucket. Press soil into the hole firmly with your hands, and water.

24. Add more soil and press in firmly. Water again.

25. Soil in the border should be at the same level as the soil in the pot. You may have some soil left in the muck bucket. Save for later uses.

26. Gently step on soil around plant to position it firmly in place. Mark with your own plant marker and indelible ink.

27. Repeat steps 18–26 to plant all perennials, moving along the back, then the middle, and finally the front of the border.

28. When finished planting, reserve any leftover soil removed from the holes for future use. Place stones removed from the bed in empty plastic containers and reserve for future use when planting pots. Save all empty plastic containers for recycling; many nurseries accept their own empty nursery containers back for reuse.

29. The next morning, water your new bed to a depth of 1 inch (if it did not rain). Place a gauge in the bed and set the sprinkler as needed. Going forward, this new bed will require 1 inch of water per week, either from rain or from sprinkling. (See "Water Wisely," page 57.)

CONQUERING BY DIVIDING

Believe it or not, your baby perennial bed is going to grow up one day. In about four years, you will need to divide your perennials to keep them strong and blooming well. You'll know when a plant needs dividing if it has become a border bully, shouldering aside other plants. Also, some perennials acquire a midlife, soft-in-the-middle shape with reduced blooms. Division, like a diet, will restore youthful vigor.

Early spring or early autumn is a good time for perennial division. Use a shovel to dig up the entire root ball and plop this into a waiting muck bucket. Move out of the border and place the dug plant on a small tarp to divide. Some perennials practically fall apart, while others must be divided with a hacksaw. Sometimes it is very physical work. Cut away and discard any worn-out pieces. Wrap good pieces in wet newspaper and place aside in a shady area.

Replant a good chunk of the perennial in its original position, using extra soil and compost to fill the rest of the hole. Leftover divisions can be given away, traded, or used to plant a new bed. Place wet-newspaper-wrapped divisions inside plastic pots for support. Replant as soon as possible.

EIGHTEEN

Add Annuals

WHAT'S THE PAYOFF?

This small project shows you how to add annuals to enliven your garden mix. Annuals are a vital part of the North American mixed border. Here we will go far beyond impatiens and marigolds (although there is not one thing the matter with these two lovable favorites) to explore an array of very easy-to-grow annual delights. Annuals have been called the jellybeans of the garden, and this project reveals how you can enjoy these cheap and cheerful treats by the handful.

With the way the weather works in this country, perennials simply can't be counted upon to provide all the color and excitement that a garden needs. An English peony may bloom for a long, cool, drizzly month in London, but that scenario is more unlikely here when May's temps can blast up to 80°F. Annuals are America's answer to the slambang border. They are also the answer to a container gardener's prayers. No matter where or how you garden in this country, annuals are a treat that you should never deny yourself.

Since the annuals described here are not fussy to grow, the larger part of this project consists of annotated sidebars describing many different types of annuals. You'll see that some I've included are perfumed, some are vines, some have crazy-colored foliage, and some leave intriguing seed heads.

Where I live in Zone 5, I purchase many tender annuals as nursery-pack seedlings and transplant these into the garden. (These are described in the first list.) There are also very hardy annuals that I sow directly into the soil (the second list). Some plants appear in both lists because I can transplant seedlings for early flowers and sow seeds to extend the flowering season until late autumn. The third list is of annuals that reliably self-sow every year in Zone 5 and decorate my garden in free-form splendor. All annual seed packets have information regarding when to plant where you live. Annuals are very easy to manage, both horticulturally and budget-wise.

In the past I sowed flats of tender annuals inside the house for transplanting into the garden later. Frankly, I don't do much of that anymore because seed flats need constant attention. Although it is so tempting to get a jump on the season by germinating seeds inside, unless you have fantastic light and time to care for those babies twice a day, you are wasting your time.

However, my local nursery will germinate and raise seedlings for me. I give them the seeds and they use their professional equipment (and staff) to raise the seedlings. I then purchase the number of seedlings that I want and they sell the rest to their other customers. This genius solution shows great garden cooperation of the first tier, and I bet your local nursery will go for it, too.

If your garden is located in a warm part of the country and has a long growing season, you can sow many tender annuals directly into your garden. Your rate of subsequent self-sowing will also be greater. In fact, you may need to ascertain with some annuals that you aren't creating a takeover situation on your home turf. Thankfully, all nurseries and

TENDER ANNUALS THAT TRANSPLANT WELL

CLEOME	*3 feet tall; pink, white, or purple; great seedpods*
LOVE-LIES-BLEEDING	*2 feet tall; long reddish chenille tassels*
FLOWERING TOBACCO	*some up to 4 feet tall, others shorter; look for perfumed types*
LARKSPUR	*annual delphiniums; fantastic blues, whites, and pinks (these are the more compact one-season wonders that are related to the taller, fussier perennial delphiniums)*
CALENDULA	*antique medicinal plant; wonderful hot colors*
MARIGOLD	*look for signet types with single flowers and scented foliage*
ZINNIA	*great colors; tall and short varieties; excellent cutting flower*
PETUNIA	*dark purple cinnamon-scented type*
POLKA DOT PLANT	*grown for pink dotted leaves; works in light shade*
PLUMED CELIOSA	*old-fashioned plant; upright plumes in hot colors*
WISHBONE FLOWER	*great in heavy shade; blue and lavender flowers*
MEXICAN SUNFLOWER	*4 feet tall; bright orange zinnia-like flowers*
JOSEPH'S COAT	*grown for tricolored leaves*
SNAPDRAGON	*flowers in almost every color; some taller than others*
BROWALLIA	*blue flowers; perfect in deep shade*
DUSTY MILLER	*matte-silvery foliage; great accent with other colors*
COSMOS	*5 feet tall; airy foliage; flowers in pink, red, white, and bright yellow*
CALIFORNIA POPPY	*threadlike foliage and many different hot-colored flowers; great seed heads*
HELIOTROPE	*dark purple; delicious scent; old-fashioned plant*
STATIS	*odd, winged foliage; flowers can be cut and dried for winter use*
SWEET ALYSSUM	*purple, white, or lavender; low-edging plant with honeylike fragrance*
THUNBERGIA	*vine climbs about 5 feet; pale orange, yellow, or white flowers with dark eyes*

HARDY ANNUALS TO SOW DIRECTLY INTO THE GARDEN

Yes, the terms "tender" and "hardy" are so loose they rattle at times. You will see some overlapping here due to the imprecise nature of the terms.

CLEOME	*page 133*
LOVE-LIES-BLEEDING	*page 133*
SWEET PEA	*old-fashioned climbing vines; sweetly perfumed flowers in every color of the rainbow; wonderful for tiny vases (the annual vine is not invasive, but beware of the perennial sweet pea)*
GOURD	*exuberant climbers; white flowers and multicolored fruit*
MORNING GLORY	*old favorite; great climbing vine; look for unusual colors and markings resurrected from old gardens*
RUNNER BEAN	*familiar vegetable plant; beautiful scarlet, pink, or yellow flowers (and beans!)*
LARKSPUR	*see page 133*
LOVE-IN-A-MIST	*delicate threadlike foliage; intricate, almost turquoise flowers; great seed pods*
NASTURTIUM	*either bush or vining; loves very poor soil; flowers and leaves in many different colors; flowers edible*
CORNFLOWER	*silvery foliage; 2 feet tall or taller; blue, pink, purple, or white flowers*
CALIFORNIA POPPY	*see page 133*
HYACINTH BEAN	*climbing vine; pink flowers and very shiny dark purple ornamental beans*
SCABIOSA	*delicate foliage; pincushion flower in pastel colors; airy plant*
JOHNNY-JUMP-UP	*very early flowers; old-fashioned favorite*
SHIRLEY POPPY	*delicate, very beautiful silklike flowers in all colors*
ATRIPLEX	*early spring, old-fashioned red-foliage plant; 4 feet tall; great seed heads*
PERILLA	*follows atriplex as red-foliage plant for garden; lasts until frost; tan skeletons and seed heads persist in winter garden*
IMPATIENS	*jewel-weed; tall types with yellow, orange, pink, white, or blue flowers*

seed catalogs now report upon locally invasive plants, but if you are ever in doubt, contact your local agricultural extension agent.

PURCHASE PRIOR TO INSTALLATION

- Seed packets for hardy annuals to be sown directly into garden. Purchase them as early as possible, either in late winter or early spring. Read sowing period on packets and mark top of packets with dates on Post-it notes. File seed packets in a small box in chronological planting order with dates visible.
- Nursery packs of tender annuals for transplanting. Purchase at least 6 of each plant, 12 of the smaller types. Nursery packs are available locally, from big-box stores all the way down to your local farm market. When you see nursery packs displayed outside, it is the correct planting time for your area.

TOOLS

- Small box
- Post-it notes
- Plant marker and indelible-ink pen
- Trowel
- Scissors

INSTALLATION

1. For sowing hardy annuals: Follow planting times and directions on individual packets. Sow seeds in large groups, as many little look-alike seedlings popping up together will tell you that these are your annuals, not random weeds. Trace a line in the soil around your sow-

RELIABLE SELF-SOWERS

These plants, described on pages 133–134, self-sow reliably in Zone 5 and above. They may also occasionally self-sow in colder zones (Zone 4 and below) and in favorable micro-climates near stone walls, house foundations, or other cozy spots. My advice is to not worry too much about zones here, as annuals work hard to flower wherever they are planted. It is, after all, their only chance to reproduce.

- *larkspur*
- *love-in-a-mist*
- *cornflower*
- *scabiosa*
- *Johnny-jump-up*
- *atriplex*
- *perilla*
- *annual poppies (Shirleys revert to red)*
- *impatiens: tall types self-seed; short ones do not*

FOLLOW-UP CARE FOR ANNUALS

Save the plastic plant tags and their cultural information in your garden journal. Don't place these ugly tags in the garden. Use a wooden plant marker if you can't remember the plant's name.

Although it is hard to make yourself do this simple task, pinch back annual plants as per packet and tag directions. This action promotes multiple branches, and the more branches you have, the more flowers you get.

ing area and place a plant marker in that space. This will also remind you what went where and you will be less likely to mistake your seedlings for weeds. Save the seed packets. Directly on the packet, note the sowing date and, later, the germination rate. Also note the satisfaction level at the end of the season. Paste these packets with their notes in your garden journal. *(See "Record Your Progress," page 32.)*

2. Transplanting tender annuals: Tender annuals usually die if placed in the garden too early. If a rogue late frost threatens, keep nursery

To prolong blooming, dead-head annuals regularly until near the end of the bloom season. At that time, allow some flowers to set seed. Leave seed heads in the garden as long as possible (all winter is great) to promote self-seeding.

packs in a protected area and drape them with row cover at night. Prior to transplanting, water the nursery packs deeply and let sit for a few minutes. Use scissors to cut the thin plastic sides away and carefully pull the small plant out sideways by its root ball. Unloosen any tightly wound roots and plant the annual into a small hole at the same depth as it was in the pack. Firm in the soil. Cluster plants in groups of 6 or more.

NINETEEN

Slip In Some Shrubs

WHAT'S THE PAYOFF?

This small project introduces you to a selection of beautiful, easy-to-grow shrubs and shows you how to plant them in your garden. Many shrubs suggested here have more than one season of beauty, some boasting fragrant flowers, pretty foliage, autumn colors, interesting winter shapes, and branches to cut for forcing or for bouquets.

Shrubs, multi-stemmed woody plants, add year-around substance to your mixed borders, boosting areas where annuals and perennials do the disappearing act in winter. A great shrub, especially if it has interesting bark, graceful form, or great flowers and fruits, can be used as a specimen plant all by itself or as a textured backdrop for annuals and perennials. Shrubs make up part of what fancy gardeners call the "bones" of a landscape. Other projects in this book touch upon shrubs ("Choose the Right Roses," page 164, and "Hedge Your Bets," page 104, are two), but this section gets into the bigger world of shrubs. (Just so you know: It's a bit uncouth to call shrubs "bushes." This is true also for calling your lovely soil "dirt." Aren't you glad you have someone to tell you these important things?)

There is not one thing wrong with forsythia, mauve rhododendrons, and topiary evergreens, but since there are thousands of other worthy shrubs, you might want to look a bit further before plunking down your cash. Once you know a thing or two, you can head off to the nearest nursery or keep your eyes open when visiting the Mega-Home-Store. As long as the shrub looks healthy and bug free, you can decide for yourself where to spend your cash. I have purchased shrubs from mail-order sources, but since these must be packed in boxes and shipped, they are usually much smaller than the potted ones for sale in nurseries. Shrubs are pricier than other garden plants, so it's more satisfying to pick out something that looks good right away than having to wait years before it grows and has a presence.

Besides your budget, there are a few other considerations when purchasing specimen shrubs for your garden. First, be sure to look at the tag and believe it when it says that the plant may reach a diameter of 15 feet. If you're looking for something smaller, keep looking. Second, stick to your own zone or your shrub will die during the winter. Yes, camellias are really great, but only in warm Zones 8 to 10. Thirdly, do read the tag to see if your shrub wants sun or shade. A sun-loving baby is just going to look spindly and bare under your maple. Choose something else.

Included in this project is an annotated list of 25 great shrubs. Choose as many shrubs as you have space for, and can afford, and slip some into your garden today.

READ THE TAG BEFORE PLANTING

HYDRANGEA — *large genus; interesting flowers; long-lasting flowers can be dried; look for oak leaf (Zones 5–9) or peegee (Zones 3–8)*

KERRIA — *yellow spring flowers; look for variegated leaves (Zones 4–9)*

VIBURNUM — *fragrant flowers; good berries; autumn color (various zones by type)*

VITEX — *6 feet tall; long-lasting blue flowers (Zones 6–9)*

WITCH HAZEL — *late-winter flowers; great autumn foliage; check species for zone hardiness*

BROOM — *fragrant flowers; European favorite (Zones 5–9)*

SMOKEBUSH — *old-fashioned filmy flowers; look for red-leaved (Zones 5–8)*

FOTHERGILLA — *scented spring flowers; great autumn color; forces easily (Zones 4–8)*

ITEA — *spring flowers; great autumn color; likes shade (Zones 5–9)*

PUSSY WILLOW — *look for black with red stems; great in winter and for forcing (Zones 5–8)*

DAPHNE — *look for 'Carol Mackie'; early-spring flowers; very fragrant; variegated leaves (Zones 4–8)*

SHADBUSH — *white spring flowers; blue berries; nice autumn color; good for forcing (Zones 4–9). Some references call shad a multi-stemmed small tree.*

CORYLOPSIS — *fragrant yellow flowers in spring; nice shape; forces well (Zones 5–8)*

PIERIS — *evergreen; pink or white flowers; some with new red leaves (Zones 5–8)*

MOCK ORANGE — *heavenly fragrance; white flowers; big plant (Zones 4–8)*

POTENTILLA — *small-size plant; yellow flowers (Zones 2–7)*

INDIAN HAWTHORNE — *evergreen; many pink flowers (Zones 8–10)*

SPIREA — *look for golden leaves of 'Gold Flame' or old-fashioned 'Bridal Wreath'; latter forces well (Zones 3–8)*

TAMARISK — *airy foliage and pink feathery flowers; strong as an ox (Zones 2–9)*

WEIGELA — *many flowers; look for golden-leaved, nice form (Zones 5–8)*

LILAC — *flowers in white, pink, or purple; fragrant; zone depends upon species*

ABELIOPHYLLUM — *many very early pinkish white flowers; fragrant; forces well (Zones 5-8)*

BEAUTY-BERRY — *pink flowers; many interesting berries (Zones 5–8)*

MAGNOLIA — *try stellata; many starry white flowers before leaves (zones 3–8)*

BUCKEYE — *big-size plant; fuzzy spikes of white or red flowers (Zones 4–8)*

PURCHASE PRIOR TO INSTALLATION

- Shrubs suitable for your garden space and climate; buy at least 2 your first time
- Compost (if you don't have your own)

TOOLS

- Shovel for digging hole and moving soil
- Muck bucket

INSTALLATION

1. Decide shrub location. A position in a mixed border offers regular watering and protection from lawn mowers. Eyeball eventual size at maturity for suitability of location.

2. Dig a hole with the shovel. Make the hole a bit deeper than the shrub container and twice as wide as the root ball.

3. Place the soil from hole in the muck bucket.

4. Water the hole and let it soak in.

5. Place two handfuls of compost in the hole.

6. Water again.

7. Press down firmly on the compost in the hole to pack it.

8. Add soil from bucket and water. Press firmly.

9. Remove the shrub from the pot. *Do not* pull out by stems, as this damages the plant. Knead the pot or roll it firmly on the ground to loosen roots and persuade the shrub from the pot.

10. If the roots are spiraling around, tease them apart with your fingers so that they can be spread out. If necessary, use scissors to cut a few roots apart.

11. Plant the shrub at the same depth as it was in the nursery container. Although some of the soil from the sides and bottom of the container may fall away, you should not cover the top of the root ball

HOW TO FORCE SHRUB BRANCHES INDOORS

Impatient for a touch of spring? In late winter, sometime around the end of February, cut branches from forsythia, pieris, abeliophyllum, pussy willow, corylopsis, and/or spirea. Soak branches in a bathtub of warm water to rehydrate bud scales. Arrange each type in separate vases and place in a cool location out of direct sunlight. Flower and leaf buds will open gradually. Keep water clear and sweet by simply flushing it out in the sink as needed.

BEFORE SHRUBS

with any additional soil. (It was planted at its proper depth in its container.) Backfill the bottom and sides of the hole with soil if necessary to keep the top of the root ball in its proper position.

12. Water the plant in the hole and alternate adding soil, water, and firming with your hands. This makes root development more likely. Use the soil from the container and mix it freely with soil you removed from the hole. Place leftover soil in your compost pile.

VIBURNUM   SMOKE BUSH   VITEX

KERRIA

HYDRANGEA

AFTER SHRUBS

13. When the hole is filled, create a little circular dam around the drip line of shrub so that water trickles in instead of running off.

14. Newly planted shrubs require spot watering until established. *(See "Water Wisely," page 57.)*

TWENTY

WHAT'S THE PAYOFF?

This medium-sized project shows you how to choose one, or several, trees to add to your garden and, most important, tells you how to make your trees happy. A tree in just the right spot, with just the right exposure, and in just the right climate is a happy tree. In this project you will learn about unusual but easy-to-grow trees that add a lot more to your landscape than mere green leaves. You will also see that there are small trees that add color and form to the back of the mixed border. Trees are the fourth essential cornerstone in creating a garden, with perennials, annuals, and shrubs discussed in the previous projects forming the other three essentials. These four cornerstones make a well-balanced landscape that provides color, form, and texture in ongoing waves of spectacular plant performances.

A tree has various tasks to perform in your garden besides just standing there. Your chosen tree should offer at least two seasons of beauty, its

TREE QUESTIONS

Answer these questions and take the information with you when you visit your nursery tree specialist. If you don't know an answer, take the question to the specialist. Most know their geographic area well.

- *Is your location sunny, shady, or very windy?*
- *What kind of soil do you have? (If you're not sure, take a potful with you to the nursery.)*
- *Is your property a wetland?*
- *Is your property exceptionally dry?*
- *Is your future tree site in a frost pocket? (Frost rolls down a hill like water. Very early-spring-blooming trees will suffer in a frost pocket.)*
- *Does your nursery guarantee its tree stock? Under what conditions? For how long?*
- *How big is your garden space and how tall do you want your tree to grow? Do you need it to grow quickly or slowly?*
- *Does your nursery deliver? Does it plant? What is the fee for each? Is tipping nursery workers standard practice?*

INTERESTING TREES

Ask your tree expert about the suitability of these unusual but agreeable trees.

SOURWOOD	*Zones 5–9; to 30 feet; white flowers; showy seed capsules; red fall color*
MAGNOLIA	*'Betty' Zones 3–8, 10 feet, purple flowers, deciduous; 'Saucer', Zones 4–9, 30 feet, huge pink flowers before leaves appear; 'Star', Zones 3–8, 20 feet, white, multi-petaled flowers before leaves appear; 'Brachen's Brown Beauty', evergreen, 30 feet, leaves velvety brown on underside, white flowers*
GOLDEN CHAIN TREE	*Zones 5–7; 15 feet; long drooping flower clusters like wisteria but yellow, graceful, small leaves*
JUNIPERS	*Zones 3–9; evergreen; various heights including prostrate; look for weeping or pyramidal, or columnar*
FRANKLINIA	*Zones 5–9; 15 feet; white camellia-like flowers in late summer; sometimes still in flower when leaves turn red for fall*
DOVE TREE	*Zones 6–8; 20 feet; beautiful white birdlike flowers*
CYPRESS	*various zones, mostly warm; 30 feet; good tall pointy evergreen*
HAWTHORNE	*Zones 5–7; 20 feet; white clouds of flowers; red fruit*
REDBUD	*Zones 4–9; 20 feet; lavender flowers on bare branches followed by heart-shaped leaves; yellow fall color; also a purple-leaved form*
HAZEL	*Zones 4–7; from 10 feet to 40 feet; contorted type has small twisted branches; otherwise pyramidal; great catkins in spring; yellow fall foliage*
DOGWOOD	*Zones 5–9; 20 feet; showy white flowers; red fruit; deep red fall foliage*
CORNELIAN CHERRY	*Zones 4–8; 20 feet; yellow spring flowers; many red edible fruits in fall*
ARBORVITAE	*Zones 2–8; 40 feet; good evergreen for columns or triangular shapes*
STEWARTIA	*Zones 5–7; 20 feet; beautiful multicolored bark; white flowrs in summer; orange fall leaves*
MOUNTAIN ASH	*Zones 3–6; 20 feet; very showy berry clusters in autumn; airy foliage*
SNOWBELL	*Zones 5–8; 25 feet; fragrant white flowers*
CHINESE QUINCE	*Zones 6–8; 20 feet; beautiful multicolored bark; pink flowers; softball-sized yellow fruit*

FRINGE TREE	Zones 3–9; 20 feet; tasseled white flowers; perfumed; berries
CALIFORNIA INCENSE CEDAR	Zones 5–8; 40 feet; a narrow spire-making evergreen
LACEBARK PINE	Zones 4–8; 30 feet; gorgeous multi-colored bark on a beautiful evergreen
PURPLE-LEAVED PLUM	Zones 3–8; 20 feet; small pink flowers and deep purple leaves
JAPANESE MAPLE	Zones 5–8; 20 feet; cut leaves; lateral shape; fantastic fall color
SHADBUSH	Zones 4–9; 20 feet; white flowers; blue fruit; good fall color (sometimes classified as a shrub)
CRABAPPLE	Zones 5–8; 15 feet; pink buds; white flowers; yellow fruits
PARROTIA	Zones 4–8; 20 feet; beautiful multi-colored bark; orange and yellow fall leaves
RIVER BIRCH	Zones 5–7; 60 feet; orange and tan bark; graceful foliage; yellow fall leaves
HARDY SILK TREE	Zones 6–9; 25 feet; lacy foliage; fluffy pink powder-puff flowers in summer; long seed pods

shade should be a welcome feature, its breadth and height should look pleasing in your space, and it should be part of the hospitality that you offer to birds—either in the way of shelter or as a food source.

Trees are an investment in your landscape, and whenever I am shelling out more moolah than usual, I want to talk to an expert about my purchase. Therefore, the advice from here is to go to a reputable local nursery to purchase a tree. The local Home-Mega-Store nursery will have trees that are perhaps less expensive, but no one there is going to help you pick the right tree for you. Most good nurseries employ tree experts and guarantee their stock. Most nurseries deliver, too, a consideration if you don't have a truck.

Below is a list of questions you will need to answer before you go to your local nursery to consult with their tree expert. These are points that will help the expert focus upon your tree possibilities. The wrong tree can cost you far more than its original purchase price. For example, removing an unwanted, overgrown tree can easily cost two thousand dollars, a princely sum that most gardeners would rather invest in garden furniture or a new patio.

That frightening note sounded, there is nothing like planting a tree on your property for posterity. Every day, my husband drives past white birches he planted as a child. An acorn my son sprouted and planted (for my previous book, *Forcing, Etc.*) is now a nine-foot-tall oak. And here in chilly New York, our entire family looks forward to the huge Bette Midler–like blooms of our pink saucer magnolia every spring.

I have included a long, annotated list that tells you about a variety of unusual but beautiful tree choices. This group also includes the ever-fascinating realm of evergreens that make winter so gorgeous. Peruse the list and discuss possible choices with your nursery.

Finally, the how-to part of this project tells you the proper way to plant a tree. This is not a complicated process, but does require a strong back. If tree planting is not a good activity for you, ask your nursery if they will deliver and plant your tree. Most do this for a minimal fee.

PURCHASE PRIOR TO INSTALLATION

- Tree: either bound and burlapped or in a very large container

TOOLS

- Shovel
- Muck bucket
- Bamboo garden stakes: 2

INSTALLATION

1. Place the tree on its site and prop upright with a shovel. (If you dis-covered at the nursery that you cannot lift your chosen tree, con-sider paying for delivery and installation. An injured back can ruin your garden year.)
2. Step away and observe the tree from a distance. Is the best side showing? If not, rotate the tree and look again.
3. When you're satisfied with the placement, move the tree to the side.
4. Use the shovel to remove sod from the tree planting spot.
5. Put the sod in compost pile. Do not use it to refill the hole after planting. Decomposing sod leaves underground holes deadly to tree roots.
6. Use the shovel to dig soil and make a planting hole. Place soil in a muck bucket.
7. Use a stick to measure the width of the root ball and the other stick to measure the depth.
8. Diameter of the hole should be at least 5 times the width of the tree trunk.
9. Depth of the hole should be the same size as the root ball. The top of the root ball must be level with the surrounding ground.
10. If the tree is burlapped, do not remove the burlap from the root ball.
11. Gently place the tree in the hole. Do not drop the tree in as this may sever the roots.
12. Loosen and pull back the top of the burlap. Cut away any wire used

STEPS 7, 8, 9 & 10

STEPS 11, 12, 13 & 14

STEPS 19 & 20

ETC...

to bind the tree. Reach into the hole and cut away as much rope and twine as possible. Leave burlap intact. It will rot away eventually.

13. If the tree is potted, water thoroughly and let it sit for a few minutes to loosen up. Press and roll the container on the ground to loosen the soil. Do not pull the tree out by its trunk. Coax it out gently.

14. Gently set the tree in the hole. Do not damage the roots.

15. To ensure that tree is straight, step away and dangle a bamboo stick, like a golfer dangles a club, to "read the land." Eyeball the stick against the tree trunk from several sides to ensure that it is not leaning.

16. Refill the hole with soil from the muck bucket. Do not add amendments. Arborists now agree with research showing that trees must cope with their existing conditions to truly thrive.

17. Firm the soil with your feet, taking care to avoid damaging any shallow roots.

18. When the hole is level with the surrounding ground, use your hands to create a small dam around the tree trunk. This will keep water from running away.

19. Mulch soil with coarse wood chips in a wide, solid circle around the tree. This helps conserve water and keeps lawn mowers away.

20. Water, water, water. Use a mere trickle from the hose applied at ground level, but water at least 5 gallons twice weekly. To measure 5 gallons, trickle hose into a 5-gallon bucket and time how long it takes to fill. That's how long to trickle water onto your new tree. Ample water is the most important factor to a newly planted tree's survival.

21. There is no need to stake your tree. Unstaked trees develop stronger root systems, so do not do it.

22. Do not fertilize your tree. It is not necessary.

23. Get to know your local tree person. Leave pruning and any pest or disease issues to the care of professionals. This is one big way to please your tree into long-lasting health and beauty.

TWENTY-ONE

CONTAIN YOURSELF

WHAT'S THE PAYOFF?

This small project outlines how to plant a container and the basic maintenance routine required to keep your potted plants at tip-top performance. Caring for containers is a very satisfying micro-chore within the macro-context of a larger garden. Start with a few and you'll soon discover the joys of puttering among the pots.

Actually, a better title for this project would be *"Don't* Contain Yourself."* Containers—whether they are clay pots, metal planters, wooden window boxes, mossy baskets, or old rubber boots—are the best way to accessorize your garden. A front porch with a fabulous collection of containers is like a great suit complemented with just the right scarf, earrings, and purse. And, just as changing accessories can make an outfit look entirely different, a fresh array of containers will make your garden always look interesting.

Containers offer opportunities to extend garden planting space, to move plants around easily, and to grow plants that need a bit of extra attention, such as an orange tree in New York, or a cactus in Alaska. Containerized plants can also be positioned in gaps in mixed borders. Some gardens are grown entirely in containers, and any urban rooftop gardener will happily testify that vegetables, trees, shrubs, bulbs, perennials, and annuals will grow in them. Even a redwood tree can be grown (for a while) in a big planter. So, please, don't contain your enthusiasm for great potted plants in the greater garden.

Please note that all the containers here are meant to be grown outside. For indoor gardening, see "Garden Indoors," page 285.

The key to container success is to face the fact right from the get-go that this type of gardening is different. An outdoor container will probably have to be watered every day because the soil inside, unlike the soil in a bed or border, is subject to evaporation on all sides, not just the top surface. Most containers dry out far faster than soil in garden beds.

Also, because there must be a hole or holes for drainage *(see sidebar, opposite)*, soil nutrients are going to continually run right out with the excess water. Therefore, containers must be gently fed weekly with water-soluble fertilizer to keep plants healthy and productive.

Finally, in areas of frost and freeze, containers must be protected, or they will be prone to break, spilling and killing their contents. *(See "Storage," page 158.)*

STYLE AND SUBSTANCE

Choosing containers to put in your garden is as personal as selecting any other kind of décor. It is sometimes nice to have everything match, and it is sometimes fun to mix things up a bit. Rows of perfectly matched orangerie tubs or large terra-cotta urns have a lovely formal serenity, while clusters of brightly colored glazed pots and various odd pieces can add whimsical surprises.

Although I hate to sound like a snob, cheap plastic pots rarely look charming. It takes little effort to transplant a pretty coleus out of plastic and into something nicer. The exception to this is, of course, those wonderful plastic pots, usually on a grand scale, that cannot be distinguished from terra-cotta and metal. These are invaluable on rooftops and decks where weight is an issue. Also, many are entirely freeze-proof and a boon to folks who must consider breakage every winter.

WHY DOES THERE HAVE TO BE A HOLE?

Drainage is essential for healthy plants. Containers without holes cannot support healthy plants because the roots inevitably get soggy and rot. You can try to use a container without holes (sometimes called a cachepot) by planting a plastic pot with holes that will slip inside the cachepot. However, you must con-stantly check to make sure that the water caught inside the cachepot hasn't accumulated to the point where it covers the bottom of the plastic liner pot.

You can use a nail to hammer holes in metal planters and you can try a masonry bit to drill into a clay pot, but there is a great way to use an irresistible container that has no drainage. If it is entirely leak-proof, turn this container into a water pot. Position the pot in a pretty place (a spot in a mixed border adds interest to the flowers) and fill it to the brim with water. Birds and butterflies will swoop in to sip. Tiny aquatic plants can be added, but just plain clear water is decorative enough. Simply flush water containers with the hose when murkiness or larvae appear.

PURCHASE PRIOR TO INSTALLATION

- Containers
- Plants: Plan to make some pots full of variety and color and others as a show-case for one special specimen.
- Potting soil
- Compost (if you don't have your own)
- Builder's sand: 1 bag

TOOLS

- Trowel
  or Scoop (old plastic nursery container works fine)
- Washtub or muck bucket filled with water
- Dishwashing detergent
- White vinegar, 1 quart
- Gravel, several handfuls
- Broken terra-cotta shards
- Styrofoam peanuts (optional)

INSTALLATION

1. Fill the washtub or muck bucket with water for cleaning your containers. Dunk containers in the muck bucket to wet. Remove them for soaping up.

2. Wash containers thoroughly with soap and water and rinse them with a hose.

3. If a container has been used previously, use an old pot scrubber and vinegar for gentle sterilization. Do this outside the water in the muck bucket. Try to keep the water in the muck bucket free of soap and vinegar.

4. Soak terra-cotta pots in the muck bucket (after cleaning) for at least one hour. This prevents dry terra-cotta from wicking water away from plants.

5. To plant, place a piece of broken terra-cotta pot inside the container over each drainage hole to prevent soil from pouring out.

6. Add a layer of gravel to the bottom of the container to facilitate drainage.

7. If your container is very large, add Styrofoam peanuts to adjust interior volume. These peanuts will not interfere with plant growth or drainage and allow large containers to be moved more easily.

8. To make a quick-draining potting medium, mix potting soil, compost, and sand in equal parts.

9. Use potting soil that has been thoroughly moistened. (Most bagged potting soil has been totally dehydrated and must be reconstituted as per instructions on the bag.)

10. Press layers of your mixed potting medium firmly into the container. Fluffy soil dries out too quickly and does not give roots anything to grab.

11. Occasionally, give the container a good shake to further settle the medium.

12. Water as you go to prevent dry pockets in the medium. This part is messy, like making mud pies.

13. Eyeball the size of the plant root ball intended for the new con-

tainer. The plant should be buried at the same level—no deeper and no shallower. The one exception is container-grown tomatoes. Tomatoes are always planted deeply, as the buried stem will sprout roots and make the plant more stable. *(See "Take Time for Tomatoes," page 217.)*

14. Gently tease plant roots apart before burying them in medium. If the plant has a solid mass of roots that cannot be untangled, use sharp scissors to cut 3 slits in the mass. This is to encourage the roots to grow out instead of continuing to make an unproductive knot.

15. Water the plant in and press the soil firmly around the stem.

16. Add more plants to the container as wanted.

17. Keep newly planted containers away from direct sunlight for about 1 week.

18. To maintain containers: Your containers may require daily watering during peak growth. Use your finger to check for soil moisture. Watering in the morning is always preferable to watering in the evening; yes, more water will evaporate, but less disease and fungi will appear.

19. Fertilize container plants at least once a week. Use a double dilution of water-soluble fertilizer: Instead of 1 teaspoon to 1 quart of water, add ½ teaspoon to 1 quart of water.

20. Almost all plant pests can be banished with a spritz of insecticidal soap. Do this on a cloudy day or move container to a shady spot. For persistent infestations, spray and tent with a floating row cover.

21. Container plants are fun to primp. Get in there with your pruners or scissors and make that container gorgeous. It's quick and satisfying at times when the rest of the garden may be a bit uncontrollable. You won't be able to contain your joy.

STORAGE

It is dicey to leave valued terra-cotta outside in freezing weather unless the contents are emptied and the pot turned upside-down. Concrete, wood, and metal fare better in freezing weather and will attain a patina quicker if left outside.

Tender container plants can be dragged inside for the winter. Either keep them growing in a sunny window or induce dormancy in a cool, dark basement. (Even if you have a state-of-the-art greenhouse, plants will pout when moved from outdoors inside. Expect a certain amount of leaf dropping and hysterics as those tenders adjust to life indoors.) Refrain from fertilizing during winter. Water only enough to keep plant from wilting.

You can try wrapping large, difficult-to-move containers in black plastic to protect them from break-ing. (Containers break in freezing weather when repeated doses of snow, sleet, and water expand the soil in the pot like water in an ice tray.) In my experience, plastic wrappings require winter watching as the plastic rips when exposed to freezing. Also, it looks very ugly. It is better to invest in large freeze-proof pots or to purchase a heavy-duty dolly to move containers indoors.

TWENTY-TWO

BRIGHTEN SHADY SPOTS

WHAT'S THE PAYOFF?

Some people mistakenly moan about shade in their gardens. Having a shady area is just like having mousy hair: It is only a problem if you don't brighten it and keep it nicely groomed. With this small project, you'll learn how to highlight your shade and how to keep it looking tidy. To formulate a shady garden and make it appear charming, you will need to know what plants work in shade and a few design tricks for transforming blah into beautiful. But if you prefer to forgo plants altogether, create a small shady seating area as described in "Determine a Destination," page 81.

Once you have decided that you want plants in your shade area, you need to answer this question: Can I dig a hole there? Often the soil under a big tree will be so dense with tangles of roots that it is impossible to scrape even a very shallow hole with a trowel. If this is the case, no problem: Your plants will go in pots. If your shady ground can accommodate any size hole you like, great—you can put many plants

SHADE-LOVING
PLANTS THAT
LOVE POTS

*These can also go in the
ground if you can dig holes.*

- ⚘ *coleus*
- ⚘ *ferns*
- ⚘ *caladiums*
- ⚘ *begonias*
- ⚘ *ivy*
- ⚘ *fuchsias*
- ⚘ *elephant's ear*
- ⚘ *taro*
- ⚘ *lobelia*
- ⚘ *sweet alyssum*
- ⚘ *browallia*
- ⚘ *violets*
- ⚘ *primulas*
- ⚘ *impatiens*
- ⚘ *foxgloves*
- ⚘ *pansies*

right into the soil. If you can dig holes in some areas but not in others, fine. You will have some plants in pots and some in the ground.

There are lots of fun opportunities to brighten up your shady spots. Choose pots and plant material that shine out of the shadows. Containers glazed or painted in whites, bright yellows, and chartreuse sparkle in the dark. Dark reds, blacks, browns, grays, and most matte finishes are swallowed up. Plant-wise, look for variegated leaves with white, gold, and yellow highlights. Also look for shade-loving flowers that sparkle. For example, choose white annual lobelia instead of a dark purple variety.

Here are two more shiny tricks. Fill a broad shallow container to the brim with water and place this in your shade area. The water will reflect and shimmer any bit of light that peeks in. And try this old stage trick: Position a small mirror flat on the ground like a faux little lake. This will also catch a bit of light and reflect it upward into the understory of your tree.

Shady spots often get a bit scraggly. To counteract this tendency, create a small framework of edging around the perimeter of the area to define it and set it apart. A thin layer of attractive mulch within the perimeter will instantly dispel the feeling of bare soil and untidiness.

You can make your edging and mulch area rectilinear by using garden stakes and string to lay out straight lines. There is something quite appealing about a big old tree and all its roundness standing within a tidy square space. On the other hand, an undulating area of edging and mulch has a naturalistic appearance suitable for informal situations. If this is the look you want, use your garden hose to lay out broad curves on the ground.

SHADE-LOVING PLANTS FOR IN-GROUND USE

These can also thrive in a pot. Remember, even a redwood can live in a pot for a little while.

tiarella	scilla	trillium	hellebore
hypericum	pachysandra	euonymous	ferns
amsonia	dicentra	lily-of-the-valley	hosta
violets	primulas	sweet woodruff	dog tooth violet
ivy	moss	corydalis	forget-me-nots
astilbe	lady's mantle	ajuga	columbine
foxglove	epimediums	pulmonaria	snowdrops
Solomon's seal	aconites	hydrangeas	hostas
anemone sylvestris	impatiens	jewel weed	Johnny jump-up
pansies	azaleas	mountain laurel	viburnum

Whether you want to define a geometric shady spot or a sinuous one, measure the lines you have laid out and buy enough edging to install around the entire perimeter. Next, you will sprinkle a thin layer of your chosen mulch (shredded bark, pine needles, cocoa hulls, or any other material that you like) to cover the bareness between plants. Suddenly, your shady spot has a style.

PURCHASE PRIOR TO INSTALLATION

- Edging material: either metal, bricks, Belgian block, cast cement, or whatever material you like, enough for the perimeter as described above
- Mulch: shredded bark, pine needles, cocoa hulls, etc., enough to make a very thin layer within the edging
- Compost for planting (if you do not have your own)
- Pots: white or brightly colored as described above, at least 3
- Plants: as per lists above

TOOLS

- Garden stakes and string
  or Garden hose
- Shovel and/or trowel for planting

INSTALLATION

1. If you want a rectilinear shady area: Use the garden stakes and string to lay out straight lines.
2. If you want an undulating edge: Use the garden hose to plot a curvy perimeter.
3. Remove any weeds or scraggly growth inside the perimeter.
4. Cover the soil with a very thin layer of your chosen mulch. This is simply dressing, not a real mulch.
5. If you will be digging holes for permanent plant material, see "Plant Perennial Pleasures," page 123, for how to proceed. (Note: It might be difficult to plant in groups. Just squeeze things in where you can dig a deep enough hole.)
6. Readjust mulch around new plants. Use as little as possible to allow plants to seed themselves or to produce runners and spread. This is desirable.
7. Where you cannot dig holes, prepare potted plants. Mix or match pots to your own taste. (Complete directions for planting pots are explained in "Contain Yourself," page 153.)
8. Position these pots in odd-numbered groups and vary the size for interest. To elevate a pot, turn another pot upside-down and use it as a stand. You can also put a small metal side table right in the bed and arrange a group of pots on top of and around this. Use these elements to punctuate the darkness.
9. OPTIONAL: Place a large shallow bowl of water in the area to reflect light. Or place a small mirror on the ground to reflect upward underneath plants.
10. Refluff displaced mulch.

11. Stand back, examine, and adjust.

12. When finished, refrain from watering with a sprinkler until early the next morning. Shady areas should *only* be watered in early morning to prevent rot and mildew.

13. After a few days' settling-in period, reexamine the bed. If the area still looks a little glum, consider adding one ornamental object. A pile of bleached seashells, a small, inexpensive concrete object (round ball, dove, squirrel, obelisk), or a tiny tuteur painted white might be called for. Or, if you want to add a touch of madness to the makeover, this is the one place where a shiny gazing ball just might work.

TWENTY-THREE

WHAT'S THE PAYOFF?

This large project is divided into three very manageable stages that help you choose the right roses for your garden. The first stage is fun because you get to look at lots of really beautiful roses. The goal of stage one is to have a list of at least twelve roses that might work in your garden. The second stage is fun, too, because you will research those roses. The goal of the second stage is to have a practical shopping list of roses to take to your local nursery. The third stage is really, really fun, because when you're finished, five brand-new, well-chosen roses are planted and ready to bloom their heads off in your garden.

While roses are arguably the most appealing flowers in the world, they are also tops on many gardeners' anxiety lists. Most of us are willing to gloss over our little disappointments with dianthus or laugh off last summer's disastrous phlox flop, but experiencing anything less than perfectly healthy, robust roses leaves many with rounds of anguished hand-wringing.

But hand-wringing is not an option for gung-ho gardeners. When we want something in our garden, we figure out how to go about getting what we want. The trick to rose success is very simple: Great roses are roses that are right for their garden. The right roses are not fussy, they resist diseases and pests, they overwinter without extra protection, and they produce blooms that cause swoons. Walk yourself through the three stages presented here and you'll soon be famous for your rose displays.

Stage one of choosing the right roses is to buy a small notebook and visit one or two great rose gardens. Although most cities of any size can boast of a public park with roses, it is worth a day trip to visit a botanic garden when the rose garden is in bloom. It is important to visit a botanic garden as close to your zip code as possible, because you want to look at roses that might be candidates for your garden.

Botanic gardens are mandated to educate the public. Not only do they display wonderful plants, they also tell you exactly what those plants are. Every botanic garden I have visited tags every plant they have. This is where your notebook comes in handy. Plus, if you have not traveled too far afield, the roses that you see here could possibly grow in your garden. You can also ask the gardeners questions. Every time I have gotten the courage to do this, I have had a wonderful conversation and learned new tips.

Plan to arrive at your chosen botanic garden as early in the morning as the gates open. Wander in the rose garden and write down the names of roses that you like. Try to find a mixture of plants—shrubs, ramblers, and climbers—and besides jotting down names, include a brief description and comments like "'Bobby James', white multi-flowered, climbs very high, to go up gingko tree??" Your goal is to leave the garden in a state of rose bliss with the names of a dozen roses that you want to have in your garden. A dozen is probably too many for right now, but stage two whittles this list down to a more manageable size.

If you don't have time to visit a botanic garden, I have provided a cheat sheet from some of my own visits in years past. *(See "A Possible List of Roses for Many Zones," on page 66.)*

A POSSIBLE LIST OF ROSES FOR MANY ZONES

- 'Reine Victoria' (Zones 5–8), mid-pink, 2-inch blooms, long bloom period
- 'Linda Campbell' (Zones 3–8), red flowers, clusters, long bloom period
- 'Topaz Jewell' (Zones 4–8), yellow, very disease resistant
- 'Carefree Wonder' (Zones 5–8), petals pink inside, ivory outside, easy
- 'Alba' (Zones 3–8), single white, very fragrant, blooms twice
- 'Lady Banks' (Zones 7–10), yellow, climber, many flowers
- 'Butterfly Rose' (Zones 5–9), flowers change orange, pink, red as season progresses
- 'Wind Chimes' (Zones 4–9), pink, dainty flowers, fragrant climber
- 'Frau Karl Druschki' (Zones 4–9), white, double, blooms early summer and autumn
- 'Climbing Cecile Brunner' (Zones 4–9), pink, many flowers
- 'New Dawn' (Zones 5–9), pink, fragrant, constant blooms
- 'Climbing Iceberg' (Zones 5–9), white, fragrant, blooms constantly
- 'Paul's Himalayan Musk' (Zones 5–9), pink, clusters of flowers, climbs 30 feet
- 'Blanc Double de Coubert' (Zones 4–9), white, fragrant, semi-double
- 'Sara van Fleet' (Zones 3–8), big pink flowers, fragrant
- 'Wild Spice' (Zones 4–8), white semi-double, very fragrant

Once you have a preliminary list—either yours or mine or a combination of the two—stage two involves refining these notes into a rose-shopping list to take to your local nursery.

Most experienced gardeners will tell you that reading is an invaluable garden tool. Perusing a few books will take you a long way down your road to really great roses.

Take your notebook and go to the library or bookstore and look up the roses on your list. You need to know each rose's zone information, its growth habit, and any caveats on susceptibility to disease or pests. Look at the photographs in the books to get a better idea of how potential roses look in different settings. Jot all this information down. Cross the fussy, the disease prone, the not-hardy-enough off your list. Life is too short and your garden time too limited to put up with reluctant roses.

Stage three of your rose hunt takes you through the point of purchase and tells you how to plant your roses. Experienced gardeners can brag about the rose bargains they find at the Mega-Home-Store, but for the novice, the anxious, or for those who keep guarantees on file, nothing beats a local, upscale nursery for your first rose purchases.

Your local nursery owner will be happy to go over the rose list you have prepared, and will probably make further suggestions and refinements. For this sort of personal attention, it is best to call ahead and ask for a good time to visit. Keep in mind that weekends are a nursery's most hectic time and that you should be ready to actually buy at least five rose shrubs at the conclusion of your consultation. Needy, nonpurchasing customers are no joy and rarely get the red carpet treatment twice. (If it is difficult for you to get to a nursery, I've listed my favorite mail-order places in the list at right. See how easy this can be?)

Once your roses arrive at your house, you're ready for the easy part: planting them.

PURCHASE PRIOR TO INSTALLATION

- Rose shrubs, bare root or potted, at least 5
- Compost, 1 big bag (if you don't have your own)

TOOLS

- Shovel
- 2 muck buckets
- Plant markers and indelible-ink pen
- Banana peels cut into small pieces

GREAT ROSE BOOKS

- The Rose Bible, *Rayford Clayton Reddell*
- Peter Schneider on Roses, *Peter Schneider*
- The Quest for the Rose, *Roger Phillips and Martyn Rix*
- Climbing Roses, *Stephen Scanniello and Tanya Bayard*
- 100 English Roses for the American Garden, *Clair Martin*

RELIABLE ROSES BY MAIL

These three websites have tremendous rose selections, helpful telephone staff, guaranteed stock, and full descriptions and photographs of almost every rose they sell.

- *Wayside Gardens, www.waysidegardens.com*
- *Jackson & Perkins, www.jacksonand perkins.com*
- *White Flower Farm, www.whiteflower- farm.com*

INSTALLATION

1. Most roses are sold bare root. Unwrap and place stubby roots in a muck bucket. Fill with water to cover the roots. Let them soak overnight. (If you have a willow tree or pussy willow shrub, cut a handful of twigs and throw them into the water. Willow twigs release a natural rooting enhancer.)

2. Decide on your rose locations. Choose a spot with as much sunshine as possible. Climbers need a trellis, fence, or tree to lean on; shrubs can be wedged into borders. (The border layout in "Plant Perennial Pleasures," page 123, includes spaces for roses.)

STEPS 3 & 4

DIG HOLE DEEP ENOUGH & WIDE ENOUGH TO SPREAD OUT ROOTS.

STEPS 6 & 7

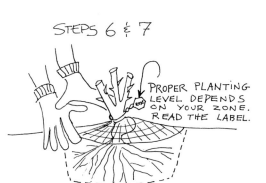

PROPER PLANTING LEVEL DEPENDS ON YOUR ZONE. READ THE LABEL.

3. To plant your rose, use the shovel to dig a big hole. Place the soil from the hole into the second muck bucket.

4. Fill the hole with water from the hose and let that soak in.

5. Place 2 handfuls of compost in the hole and mix in soil from the muck bucket. Press firmly with your hand. Water again.

6. Repeat step 5 until the hole is refilled to correct planting depth. The proper planting hole allows the stubby roots to spread out sideways and for the graft bump to be buried as deeply as the individual rose tag specifies. Remove the rose from its soaking water and place it in the hole.

7. Add another handful of compost around the stubby roots and water again. Press firmly around the roots.

8. Add a small handful of cut banana peel to the hole to provide extra minerals that roses like (potassium and phosphorus especially).

9. Add soil from the muck bucket until the hole is filled. Tread firmly around the rose to ensure that the roots have contact with the soil.

10. Use a wooden marker and indelible ink to identify roses in the garden. Keep nursery tags and other information for your garden records.

11. Repeat until all roses are planted.

12. Avoid fertilizing for at least one month. This favors underground root growth. *(See "Rose Tonics and Tips," at right.)*

13. Spot-water roses regularly (at soil level if possible) until they are established.

ROSE TONICS AND TIPS

- *Roses like compost tea. Fill an old pillowcase with compost and soak in muck bucket full of water for at least one week. Apply the liquid to the soil under your roses.*

- *Grow garlic, leeks, chives, and ornamental onions near roses to discourage pesky Japanese beetles.*

- *To prevent and cure mildew and black spot, hand spray with this mixture: In an empty gallon milk jug, add 1½ tablespoons baking soda and 1 teaspoon Ivory liquid and fill to the top with water. Mix well and decant as needed into a sprayer bottle. Spray on an overcast day. (See "Don't Get Bugged," page 51.)*

- *Jump-start growth next spring by spreading a handful of Epsom salts around every rose.*

TWENTY-FOUR

Try Some Tropicals

WHAT'S THE PAYOFF?

This small project tells you how to start tropical bulbs indoors, how to use them in your garden, and how to dig and store them for next year. The "Three C's" presented in this project—caladiums, cannas, and colocasias—are easy to grow, widely available, and can be saved from year to year with ease. The Three C's are grown from inexpensive tubers, rhizomes, and corms sold in ordinary Mega-Home-Supply stores.

Purchase these tropical bulbs in late winter or early spring when they will be on sale in big, uninspiring bins making them seem as exciting as onions in the supermarket. But you know the inside story, so buy a bunch and store them in a warm, dark place until planting day. Tropical bulbs are best when started inside one month before your last frost date. (In my Zone 5, the last frost is end of May. I start tropicals April 30.)

Gardeners in hot areas may have already played with tropicals, but now's the time for northern gardeners to get on the bandwagon with these bold, beautiful plants. Gonzo gardeners like to have fun, and tropicals bring a feeling of fiesta to temperate-zone gardens. Come join the party!

The first tropical C is caladium. Caladiums are tuberous plants grown for their red, pink, white, cream, and green marked leaves. The arrow-shaped leaves can be as small as a couple of inches or as large as eight inches long. Caladiums adore the shade and are an unexpected pleasure when singing forth from fern beds, from the shady side of the hedge, or from pots disguising the bare areas under a big tree. *(See "Brighten Shady Spots," page 159.)*

The second C is canna. Cannas have become fashionable again in the last five or six years as gardeners have grown eager to use bright colors in their mixed borders. Cannas are big tropicals for sunny areas. Their scarlet, apricot, yellow, orange, or salmon flowers can rise as tall as twelve feet. Canna foliage is also very useful in the border and can range in color from bright green, blackish purple, almost blue, to multi-colored stripes. A single canna produces many large leaves and several tall spikes of flowers, managing to astonish even the most sophisticated gardener when so much plant comes from one rhizome.

C number three is colocasia. Colocasia is another big tropical with foliage that varies from bright green to black. The huge leaves of this plant spring up from an underground corm the size of a croquet ball. Some colocasias grow as tall as seven feet high, and when their leaves gently wave back and forth in the breeze you can see why they are often nicknamed elephant's ears. (There are many other plants also called elephant's ears.) Colocasia is happiest grown in a pot that sits in the shade, making them perfect punctuations for the porch or a happy big brother to a gathering of caladiums.

PURCHASE PRIOR TO INSTALLATION

- Caladium tubers: at least 1 dozen of 1 kind
- Small plastic starter pots: 12 for caladiums
- Cannas rhizomes: 3 of 1 kind
- Plastic nursery pots: 3 8-inch pots for cannas
- Colocasia corms: 3 of 1 kind
- Plastic nursery pots: 3 8-inch pots for colocasia
- Terra-cotta pots: 3 unglazed, large enough to slip colocasia nursery pots inside
- Large saucers: 3 glazed for pots above
- Potting soil
- Sand: to mix with potting soil
- Compost (if you don't have your own)

TOOLS

- Picnic bench, garden table, or improvised stage for setting pots on indoors
- Old newspapers
- Big mixing bowl
- Floating row cover
- Trowel

INSTALLATION

1. On planting day, move a picnic bench or garden table inside to a warm spot. A position near a radiator or heat duct is perfect.
2. Arrange newspapers on the table where you will work. Potting can get messy.
3. Mix potting soil, sand, and compost in equal parts to make a starting medium for bulbs.
4. Caladiums: Plant 1 tuber in each small plastic pot as per directions on bag. Press soil firmly onto the tuber. Water well.

5. Cannas: Plant 1 rhizome per 8-inch plastic pot as per directions on bag. Press soil firmly onto the rhizome. Water well.

6. Colocasia: Plant 1 large corm per 8-inch plastic pot as per directions on bag. Press soil down firmly onto the corm. Water well.

7. Place all pots on a bench in a warm indoor spot. Keep soil moist. Do not fertilize. Leaves should appear within two weeks.

8. After the last frost has passed, begin hardening off plants. (This activity occurs in June in my Zone 5.)

9. To harden off plants grown indoors, place outside in a very protected area when the temperature is at least 65 degrees. Drape with floating row cover for extra protection from cool breezes and hot sun. Leave plants outdoors for only two hours the first day before placing them back inside. Gradually increase the time outside for the next week until plants can safely stay outside all night.

10. The following week, remove floating row cover and allow the plants to remain outside with no protection. In Zone 5, tropicals are ready to plant outside in mid-June.

11. To plant caladiums: Caladiums require shade. Sun will burn their decorative leaves. Caladiums look best when massed together closely.

12. In your chosen spot, water all 12 pots deeply and let them sit for a few minutes. Carefully tap the plants out of their pots and bury them only as deep as they were in the pot. Water in well. Top-dress with compost. Spot-water daily until plants are established. Then follow normal bed-watering routine.

13. To plant cannas: Cannas require sun. Cannas can be massed for a big effect, but are large enough to be planted in separate spots. (There is room for tropicals in the mixed border described in "Plant Perennial Pleasures" on page 123.)

14. In your chosen spot, water pots deeply and let them sit for a few minutes. Carefully tap the plants out of their pots and bury them at same depth as they were in the pot. Water in well. Top-dress with compost. Spot-water until established, then follow normal watering routine.

15. To plant colocasias: These plants require shade and prefer for their pots to stand in shallow water. Colocasias should remain in their plastic pots, which should be slipped inside terra-cotta pots. Set the pots in glazed saucers and keep saucers filled with water. Top-dress with compost.

16. After tropicals are established, fertilize with compost tea. *(See "Fertilize Effectively" on page 38.)*

17. These Three C's are pest and disease resistant and just grow larger and happier as the summer gets hotter and hotter.

18. After the first light frost, tropicals will turn brown and wilt. This is the signal to bring them back indoors for winter storage.

19. Gently dig up caladium tubers. Do not wash. Do not cut off leaves. Place on dry newspapers in a warm indoor place until soil can be

brushed away and the leaves have completely withered. Store tubers in an old onion bag in a warm (60 degrees at least), dark place until next year's start.

20. Gently fork up canna rhizomes. Do not wash. Do not cut off leaves. Let leaves wither naturally. Place one rhizome each back in their original (empty) pots and barely cover with moistened sand. Store in a warm (60 degree) dark spot. Check occasionally and remoisten sand. Beware of rot. Start again next spring.

21. Colocasias remain in their plastic pots but are allowed to completely dry out in a warm, dark spot. Let leaves wither naturally without cutting them off. Store terra-cotta pots and saucers upside down in a dry spot to avoid breakage. To start again next year, there is no need to repot. Simply begin watering the pots slowly until the first leaves appear.

Plant Perfumes For P.M.

WHAT'S THE PAYOFF?

This medium-sized project shows you how to intensify the enjoyment of your after-hours garden by adding scintillating, wafting, evening plant perfumes that charm you into a more relaxed frame of mind. The workweek fact of life for most of us is that, from Monday until Friday, darkness usually descends upon our gardens before we do. It can be a bit frustrating to look out the office window at a glorious summer afternoon and wish to be among the roses. On the bright side, getting home after dark precludes undertaking most of the big garden chores. Instead of lamenting lost afternoon rose moments, promise yourself a guilt-free garden cocktail outside under the stars while enjoying perfumes from your own beloved patch.

The plants recommended here for nighttime perfumes are real "tossers": They do not require close sniffing or rubbing of foliage to release their magic. This freedom of perfume, as well as many of these plants' white flowers, attracts night flyers for pollination purposes. Just as butterflies cavort in your garden during the day, gorgeous moths will visit at night. I especially love large, pale green luna moths and curly-tongued hawk moths that look like baby hummingbirds. Another night visitor is the romantically named Isabella tiger moth, the grown-up stage of the snow-predicting brown and black wooly-bear caterpillar.

If you're considering an evening area, you might be interested to discover that "white for night" was a delightful garden dictum popular in Victorian days when "moonlight gardens" were the rage. These special garden areas were planted extensively with white-flowering night-perfumed plants that could be thoroughly enjoyed in the cool part of the evening. One of my favorite antique garden books, *Old Time Gardens* by Alice Morse Earle (1901), describes the expansive moonlight garden of the Hon. Ben Perley Poore in Massachusetts. I include mainly white flowers in lists here, but you do not have to limit yourself as strictly as those Victorians were apt to. In particular, don't feel obliged to decorate your evening garden as Mr. Poore did with snow-white cows, white sheep, white oxen, snowy pigeons, and albino peacocks—unless you are so inclined.

This project is heavy on lists of perfumed plant choices. (I have limited the list to plants easily obtained at the most ordinary Mega-Home-Store.) The Installation section details two ways to add night-scented plants to your garden: perfumed pots for the porch and scented additions for existing borders. *(See "Contain Yourself," page 153, and "Plant Perennial Pleasures," page 123.)*

Make a list of possible perfumers and visit your local nursery as late in the day as possible. Many stars of the night garden actually look very unappealing during the brightness of the day. For example, during the daytime, most white nicotianas look like discarded tissues. But, come sunset, these daytime droopers perk up into starry flowers that toss the

SCENTED ANNUALS
- *datura*
- *nicotiana*
- *old-fashioned petunias*
- *moonflowers*
- *evening-scented stock*
- *four o'clocks*
- *dames rocket (sometimes behaves as a biennial)*
- *bottle gourds*

most expensive-smelling perfumes this side of Paris. Purchase six of one plant rather than one of six different plants. Dotting plants around always looks stingy. Buy plenty and use them as they make scents to you.

PERFUMED PERENNIALS AND BIENNIALS

- *clove pinks*
- *phlox*
- *sweet Williams*
- *evening primrose*
- *Matilija poppy*
- *Adam's needle*
- Hosta plantaginea

PURCHASE PRIOR TO INSTALLATION

FOR PERFUMED PORCH POTS

- Clay pots: 5 mixed or matched, each at least 12 inches in diameter
- Plants: 5 different types in generous quantities to fill pots
- Potting mix
- Compost (if you don't have your own)
- Sand

FOR SCENTED BORDER ADDITIONS

- Annuals: 6 of each, 2 kinds
- Perennials: 3 of each, 2 kinds
- Shrubs: 1 or 2 as you have space to squeeze into your mixed border
- Bulbs: 12 of each

TOOLS

- Trowel
- Shovel

INSTALLATION

FOR PERFUMED POTS

1. Position your 5 clay pots on the porch, each on top of a saucer or bricks to prevent rot underneath. If by the front door, place two together on one side and three on the other side.
2. Plant as per "Contain Yourself," page 153. (This project explains how to mix the potting medium and also gives tips on arranging pots.)

3. Plant each type of plant in its own pot. For example, place all 6 old-fashioned petunias in one pot. Place 6 nicotianas in another pot. Plant 6 daturas in one really big pot. Plant 6 four o'clocks in another big pot.

4. To arrange, using plant examples as above: Place the petunia pot next to the nicotiana pot on the left side of the door. The petunias drape while the nicotianas stand taller behind them.

5. Place the datura pot and the four o'clock at the right side of the door. The four o'clocks will probably be taller than the datura.

6. Behind these, place a large pot containing a scented shrub or tree. (Tender woody plants are perfect for the porch: You can drag them inside at the hint of frost.) All the trees or shrubs here will behave well in pots for at least one season.

7. Once your potted perfumers begin to perform, you might find that you want to spread them out a bit for best results. By placing each type in its own pot, you have freedom to spread the scents around.

8. Care for pots as per the usual drill for container care on pages 156–57. The annuals should bloom all summer. The tenders can come inside before the frost and be placed in a sunny window until temperatures are warm again next spring. You may get a second bloom period indoors this winter. Lucky you.

PERFUMED SHRUBS AND TREES

- brugmansia
- gardenias
- citrus trees
- choisya
- frangipani
- viburnum
- rugosa rose
- daphne
- wisteria
- mock orange
- honeysuckle
- Russian olive
- native azaleas
- clerodendrum
- silk tree
- magnolia
- citrus
- honey locust

BULBS WITH PERFUMED FLOWERS

- *acidantheras*
- *tuberoses*
- *callas*
- *lily-of-the-valley*
- *lemon lily*
- *Casablanca lily*
- Lilium formosanum

PERFUMED ADDITIONS FOR A MIXED BORDER

1. Although the suggestion here is to add perfume near your bedroom window, if it is closed up for air-conditioning, this is a moot point. These additions can be squeezed into any existing border where scents will be enjoyed at night.

2. It is easy to squeeze in plants either near the front of an existing border or near the rear. Usually the middle is full, but sometimes a few shallow-rooted annuals can be added underneath existing roses or established perennials. (Please reread "Plant Perennial Pleasures," page 123.)

3. Annuals such as old-fashioned petunias and datura are short and can be squeezed into gaps in the front of an existing border. Use the narrowest trowel you have to make a small planting hole.

4. Gourds and moonflowers can be added to scamper up already existing rose arbors or wisteria trellises. These annuals present no danger to established perennial vines.

5. In an established border, evening stock and dame's rocket can be tucked in between other plants. Check for spaces near shrubs. Taller nicotianas (especially *N. sylvestris*) and four o'clocks happily acclimatize at the rear of an established border. These two annuals can easily grow 5 feet tall in one summer.

6. For punch, add perfumed perennials in threes. Dotting a phlox here, one over there, and another someplace else just looks stingy. Three small clove pink plants will grow into a pleasing blue-green mat at the front of the border. Three sweet Williams can go just behind the clove pinks and, in subsequent years, will seed themselves into even tinier spaces. If necessary, move something unperfumed to make room for three *Hosta plantaginea* or other desirable perfumers.

7. Using your small trowel, tuck in the summer-blooming bulbs, planting three in each hole. Lily-of-the-valley needs a front-of-the-

border location. All the rest can be positioned wherever there is a space. Acidantheras, tuberoses, and callas are tender bulbs but are inexpensive enough to repurchase each spring as needed. All the other bulbs listed on page 180 will reliably return each year with no coddling.

TWENTY-SIX

WHAT'S THE PAYOFF?

This small project shows you how to transform a burnt-out patch of lawn into a new garden feature: a colorful, blooming petite prairie. Almost every garden has a "hot spot"—a place in the lawn that seems to brown up and get crispy at the exact moment when the rest of the garden is looking wonderful. Sometimes the culprit is sandy soil underneath, a barely covered ledge of rock, a particularly exposed site, or a combination of any of those factors. Here, ornamental grasses and drought-resistant flowers, all available from any ordinary Home-Mega-Store garden center, can be let loose to create an intriguing gardening opportunity in what was once an eyesore.

My own hot spot was in the front lawn, just to the left of a long vista all the way down the border. Every year, by July 4, the sandy soil under that part of the lawn heated up and fried the grass, spoiling the entire view further on. August and September heat made the burnt spot even larger and browner and I soon learned that there was no point in dumping water and fertilizer on a hot spot. So, in my usual enthusiastic way, I schemed a Plan B that is now officially known as the petite prairie.

The prairie-making process could not have been easier. I simply stopped mowing the burnt area entirely and began transplanting ornamental grasses and heat-resistant plants (many native to the true grasslands of long ago) into the patch. The prairie plants thrived in the hot, dry soil and their shade allowed the previously burnt patch to recover a bit. An artistic bit of home-made low fencing designated this prairie as "on purpose" and delineated it from the rest of the lawn. The installation tells how I made my mini-fence, but you can improvise with ideas of your own. The fence prevents the lawn guys from mowing your prairie in its early days and it also works as a cool little design feature enclosing the "wildness" within.

Six years later, this bit of enclosed grassy wildness has year-round beauty and offers an interesting contrast to the rest of my more well-mannered borders. Best of all, my little prairie is impervious to heat and drought, it is almost maintenance free and, most wonderfully, it is an irresistible butterfly magnet. This is quite a lot of payoff to get from a Plan B!

A petite prairie begins looking nicely established within a few weeks of installation. Before you know it, you'll spend mornings watching the dew glitter on your ornamental grasses while you sip from your coffee cup and the butterflies sip from your plants.

ORNAMENTAL GRASSES FOR YOUR PRAIRIE

- Miscanthus sinensis 'Gracillimus'
- Imperata cylindrical 'Rubra'
- Pennisetum 'Moudry'
- Muhlenbergia filipes
- Muhlenbergia capillaries
- Saccharum arudinaceum
- Saccharum officinarum
- Pennisetum setaceum 'Rubrum'
- Helictotrichon sempervirens

PURCHASE PRIOR TO INSTALLATION

- Bamboo garden stakes: 3 feet long, enough to make a mini-fence to enclose the perimeter of the prairie area as per Installation steps 1 and 2 below

KATHERINE'S "PRAIRIE PLANTS"

- *native asters*
- *goldenrod*
- *milkweed*
- *yarrows*
- *sage*
- *perovskia*
- *filipendulas*
- *annual poppies*
- *blueberry bush*
- *cut-leaf sumac*
- *sedum*
- *tickseed*
- *verbascums*
- *chicory*
- *woad*
- *helianthums*
- *cleomes*
- *boltonia*
- *rugosa rose*
- *annual poppies*

- Ornamental grasses
- Drought-resistant plants

TOOLS

- Garden stakes and string for laying out perimeter
- Jute garden twine
- Pruners
- Shovel
- Trowel

INSTALLATION

1. Plan your prairie space. Use garden stakes and string to outline the perimeter of your hot spot. Your prairie can be any size or shape that pleases you. My prairie happens to be rectangular, but curves work just as well, too.
2. Measure the perimeter. You will need to purchase enough bamboo garden stakes to lay out lengthwise around the perimeter. Allow space for the "rails" of the fence to overlap. At each overlap you will require an additional half-stake (1½ feet tall) as a "post."
3. To construct the mini-fence: Arrange the bamboo stakes along the ground so that the ends overlap enough to tie together with twine. While they are still flat on the ground, tie the bamboo together along one side by wrapping the overlapping ends with twine. Wrap the twine around the bamboo several times and knot securely.
4. To make mini-fence posts: While the "rails" are still flat on the ground, cut additional bamboo stakes in half and push these into the ground at every rail joint as "posts." These upright posts will support the rails. Push the posts in far enough to be steady and straight.

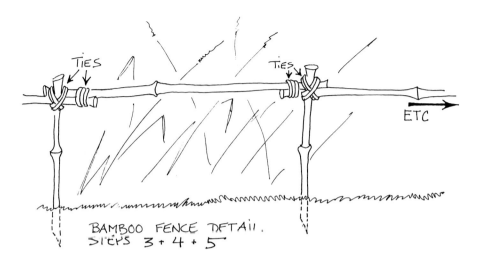

TIES

TIES

ETC

BAMBOO FENCE DETAIL.
STEPS 3 + 4 + 5

5. To erect fence: Start at one end of the railing and tie the junction of two rails to the post by wrapping and knotting the twine tightly. Move to the next post and repeat, keeping the rail as straight as possible. Slight variations look great: This is an artistic rendition of a fence, not a real fence.

6. Repeat to the end of the side.

7. Begin the next side in same manner as above and repeat until entire mini-fence encloses the proposed prairie.

8. Transplant grasses and plants into the enclosed area. Use shovel or trowel to transplant. Grasses look best as individual clumps and flowering plants as clusters of 3.

9. Sow seeds of annual poppies directly on top of the soil.

10. Do not fertilize during the first season.

11. Water 1 inch after planting is complete.

12. Water weekly until plants are established. (The prairie should receive 1 inch of water per week for the first four weeks.)

13. Do not mow inside the mini-fence. The existing burnt-out grass will eventually recover (mowing makes burning worse), and this will sprout up between plantings.

14. Mow the lawn outside the mini-fence as usual. Soon the prairie will be tall enough to assert its presence as a separate garden area.

15. Maintenance: This prairie should be left to its own wild devices throughout the growing season. The grasses and plants will bloom and self-sow their seeds. In late winter or earliest spring, set the mower on the highest setting and mow the prairie. Or weed whack carefully to avoid ripping up grass and plant crowns. Top-dress bare ground very lightly with compost or old manure. Next, allow plants and grasses to naturally re-sprout and seeds to germinate.

16. OPTIONAL: Your mini-prairie is a perfect spot to plant miniature daffs and wild tulip bulbs in autumn. Slip these small bulbs into the soil with a trowel. In spring they will bloom as the new grasses emerge. *(See "Fall into Bulbs," page 273.)*

TWENTY-SEVEN

Cultivate A Cutting Garden

WHAT'S THE PAYOFF?

This medium-sized project shows you how to plan and plant a cutting garden. It doesn't matter if your garden is ten years old and busting with flowers, it is still almost impossible to work up the moxie to harvest blooms from your beds and borders. The reason for this understandable reluctance is that, in your ornamental garden, you are always working toward having as many flowers blooming as possible at any given moment. Sure, you can sneak one or two flowers here and there without too many pangs, but what happens when you want to make a really lush bouquet? This is why most gardeners love their cutting gardens: These little agricultural zones are solely for the purpose of harvesting flowers. Make a cutting garden and you will have beaucoups de bouquets all season long.

Installing this cutting garden depends upon having a clean, grass- and weed-free bed. *(See "Make a New Bed," page 15.)* It is psychologically important that your cutting flowers be planted in rows with absolutely no

ANNUALS FOR CUTTING

- cosmos
- cleomes
- nicotiana
- Shirley poppies
- sweet peas
- nasturtiums
- larkspur
- snapdragons
- marigolds
- zinnias
- amaranth
- dahlias

CUTTING-GARDEN CANDIDATES

These perennials, all from divisions, are good for cutting

- Siberian iris
- border phlox
- coneflowers
- scabiosa
- perennial sunflowers
- rugosa roses
- feverfew
- foxgloves (true biennial)
- hollyhocks (as before)
- sweet Williams (biennial)
- lady's mantle violets

regard to what color looks best next to what other color. Remember: This is a crop area that should be arranged solely for harvest. If you start making the cutting garden look too pretty, it will become another border that you can't bear to clip.

A great place for a cutting garden is near your potager. This keeps the harvest theme going and assumes that the location is sunny and gets regular watering as needed. My cutting garden is about twenty feet long and four rows wide. (It is easy to lean in from either side to cut two rows.) I grow lots of cutting annuals, some from seed and some from inexpensive nursery six-packs. I also have a choice of fragrant old-fashioned peonies and roses stuck in my cutting garden. Finally, I have found that the cutting garden is the perfect place to save favored perennial divisions from the ornamental garden. (Information on perennial division is described in "Plant Perennial Pleasures," page 123.)

Finally, please don't let a lack of "official" flower-arranging knowledge hinder your desire for a cutting garden. I've provided tips for cutting, conditioning, and arranging on page 192, but I know that once you have your own special bouquet ingredients, you will develop your own special bouquets.

PURCHASE PRIOR TO INSTALLATION

- Annuals, either 1 packet of seeds or 12 plants, 6 kinds
- Peony, at least 2, fragrance to please your nose
- Rose, at least 1, fragrance to please your nose

TOOLS

- Garden stakes and string
- Trowel
- Shovel
- Plant markers and indelible-ink pen
- Floating row cover

INSTALLATION

1. Begin this project with a clean, weed-free bed, as described in "Make a New Bed," page 15.
2. Using the garden stakes and string, lay out the rows for your cutting garden. Long rows running south to north is the ideal row orientation.
3. With all plants still in their pots, and all seeds still in packets, plot where each type of plant will be positioned according to plant height printed on tag or packet. Tall plants must not shade short plants or emerging seedlings. In general roses, peonies,

STEPS 1 + 2 + 3 + 4

FRAGRANT PEONIES AND ROSES FOR CUTTING

This is not a cop-out: Flower fragrance is a very personal preference. I have a friend who simply adores, raves about, and swoons over the fragrance of a certain rose she grows in her cutting garden. I love my friend, but I can't stand the smell of her favorite rose. It smells really awful to me. Likewise, since our perfume preferences are so at odds, I bet that there are flowers that I love to sniff that she can't stand. Since peonies and roses are perennials, I suggest that you go to a nursery, please your own nose, and plant what you like.

STEPS 5 + 6 + 7

and divided perennials are better at the north end of the bed so as not to shade out baby plants.

4. Once all plants are arranged from south (seed-sowing area) to north (tall plants) in their rows, transplant potted plants as per instructions on the plant tags. Use the string guides to keep your rows straight.

5. Plant any perennial divisions at this north end, also. If you do not have divisions yet, consider leaving room for extending the bed later, if you wish.

6. Sow annual seeds as per instructions on the packets. Sow in straight rows to facilitate seedling recognition and weeding.

7. Mark seed rows with plant markers and include date of sowing.

8. Water the entire cutting garden 1 inch deep (as per "Water Wisely," page 57).

9. Cover areas with freshly sown seeds with floating row cover to speed germination.

10. This cutting area needs about 1 inch of water per week to stay at maximum output.

STEPS 8 + 9 + 10

11. Harvest all of your flowers either in loose bud or in full bloom. Regular picking promotes new buds and more flowers.

STEP 11

TIPS FOR ARRANGEMENTS

- *Harvest flowers very early in the morning, as this is when they are full of water and at their freshest. Cut with pruners or sharp scissors, making stems as long as possible. Place all cut flowers in a bucket of water right up to their necks. Place bucket in cool shady place and leave for at least two hours.*

- *Poppies are great for arrangements. Burn the cut end with a lighter as soon as you snip it. Then plunge it into water as described above.*

- *After the flowers are conditioned as above, remove leaves that will be under the water in the vase. Also remove any squashed petals with fingers or sharp scissors. Primp, primp, primp.*

- *For a big arrangement, place the strongest stems in the container first, crisscrossing so that you make a framework. Cut stems shorter if they are too wobbly. Add floppier flowers in between stronger stems. (You can use florist wire, foam, and frogs if you like. I don't.) Keep adding flowers until the vase is full.*

- *It is easier to make an arrangement that has a hidden back (to be placed against the wall or whatever) than it is to make an arrangement that has to look great all the way around.*

- *Once all flowers are in the container and you like the basic appearance, stick both hands (fingers spread apart) into the arrangement and fluff it up a bit just like Pamela Anderson fluffs up her hair. This secret makes arrangements look really great!*

- *An alternative way to arrange flowers is to place only one or two flowers in small vases, but to use many small vases. A line of home-grown poppies in small bottles lined up all the way down a dining table is smashing. The tiny vases can mix or match.*

- *There is no need to add anything to the water in floral arrangements. Just keep the water fresh and clean and filled to the top of the vase.*

TWENTY-EIGHT

WHAT'S THE PAYOFF?

This large project will transform a dry, rocky area of your property into a low-maintenance iris bed with plenty of visual impact. Bearded irises bloom in the interval between late spring and early summer, creating a much-needed floral transition between the end of peonies and the beginning of roses. Furthermore, irises are actually as tough as nails, so just about anytime you get the urge to take on this project, it will be fine to just get up and do it. The barren flanks of your gravel driveway, a steep dry slope of dumped fill, or the too-hot south side of a stone wall can be transformed into an iris bed in just about one weekend. If properly neglected, irises live just about forever and will burst into an early-June rainbow that will lure you out into the garden shortly after sunrise.

Iris germanica and its myriad cultivars make up the hardy, rhizomatous clan that includes the oldest cultivated European irises. These old-timers have upright fans of stiff foliage and tall straight stems sporting multiple ruffled flowers. The flowers are sea blue, maroon, tan, yellow, white, pink, lavender, dark purple, black, brown, and also come in combinations of colors. These flowers, nicknamed bearded iris, have sweet fragrances similar to Easter candy.

Bearded irises have an undeserved reputation for being fussy and short-lived. This arises from the fact that these old darlings actually resent being pampered—watered and fertilized—along with the other flowers in a border. Bearded irises make perfect candidates for gloriously holding down the fort in poor, overheated, quick-draining soil where other flowers falter.

Bed preparation for an iris interlude should not be difficult, as the point here is to choose a dry rugged spot where not much else grows. The iris spot should have lots of sun and perfect drainage. A south-facing slope is just about ideal. The bed should be at least two feet wide to allow some depth of plantings, because you do not want to have a soldierly row of irises standing at attention. The bed can be as long as you have plant material to fill. My iris interlude is tucked into a bed made where a driveway was formerly located. It is about twenty-six inches wide and thirty feet long.

Bearded irises are usually sold as a bare-root fan, with a gnarly rhizome (like a piece of fresh ginger) sporting a few stringy roots and a fan of clipped foliage. This is the least expensive way to buy irises, but you can also find them potted up in nursery containers for a bit more money. In my experience, the best time to transplant iris fans is right after their early-June bloom period, but I have moved irises around whenever I felt moved myself, and they have always lived to tell the tale. A June planting gives the shallow roots a full season to reach into the soil and grab on, making winter watchfulness much less arduous. (Any plant going through its first winter needs to be watched, as it will be susceptible to heaving itself out of the ground during freezing and thawing cycles. If you spot a heaved plant, simply cram it back into its spot.)

MATERIALS TO PURCHASE PRIOR TO INSTALLATION

- Bearded iris rhizomes, at least 25 total, 5 each of different colors *(See sources at right.)*

TOOLS

- Standard standing cultivator
- Hand cultivator
- Sharp knife
- Rubbing alcohol in a small bowl
- Scissors
- Trowel

INSTALLATION

1. Use the standing cultivator to prepare the iris bed. Scratch up and remove any straggling weeds, but don't remove gravel or stones. If the soil is very sandy, all the better. Use the hand cultivator to smooth the surface and pat the soil firmly down with your hand. Do not add compost or fertilizer to this bed. Irises like it tough.

2. Begin at the back of one end of your bed and plant toward the front, moving along the bed when you have filled one section with rhizomes. Plant in staggering lines with each rhizome about a foot away from the next.

3. Examine each bare-root rhizome before planting. Use very clean scissors to remove unsightly foliage and to create a nice crisp fan. If any parts of

WHERE TO OBTAIN BEARDED IRISES

Without a doubt, my favorite place to obtain irises is from another gardener. Feel free to ask for rhizome divisions after flowering is finished, because any good gardener knows that dividing makes irises bloom better. (Step 14 on page 197 explains how to divide irises.)

My next favorite place is from the wonderful Schreiner's Iris Gardens in Salem, Oregon (800-525-2367 or www.schreinersgardens.com). This family-run nursery is one of the best in the country. Their irises are hardy, happy, and inexpensive.

HEALTHY IRIS RHIZOME

the rhizome are moldy or mushy, cut these off with a sharp knife. After every cut, clean the knife with alcohol to avoid spreading diseases from one plant to the next.

4. It is key to your iris success that you resist the urge to bury that fat rhizome. That part of the iris sits on top of the soil. Only the roots are buried. The easiest way to bury the roots is to use the trowel to create a small mound (slightly higher than the bed) that has a small dry moat around it. Perch the rhizome on the mound and, with your hand, arrange the roots into the dry moat and cover them with the soil that has been pushed aside. That's it!

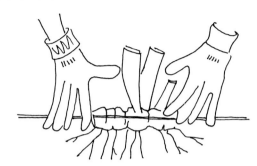

PROPER PLANTING LEVEL FOR IRiS RhiZOMES

5. Irises are planted so shallowly that they tend to fall over until their roots grow. You can prop the fan up with a few pebbles, but do not add more soil on top of the rhizome. Just be more stubborn about making the iris stand up than the iris is about falling over.

6. Move along to the next spot and dig the next little mound and moat. Occasionally you may accidentally uproot a neighboring fan, but no harm is done—just rearrange the roots and replant.

7. After you have planted all your fans, gently sprinkle the iris bed with water and be prepared to reprop any fans that fall over. Irises need a little water to start growing in their new beds, but bearded irises hate being soggy.

8. Keep any stray weeds and leaves out of the bed, as this keeps water at the rhizome. Water only when it has been extremely hot and dry during this first growing season. No watering is needed in subsequent years.

9. Some of the fan foliage will die back during the summer. This is normal and you can hand-groom or not as you choose.

10. Do not mulch your iris bed. Spring-planted irises are much better at getting through the winter without heaving up, despite their shallow systems. Mulch is very bad for this type of iris.

11. You can expect many of your irises to bloom the following June. Different types bloom at different times, so you should have waves of bloom that last up to three weeks. Visit your irises every morning and be sure to smell their wonderful perfumes. Look how their little beards colorfully welcome bees to crawl inside the flowers.

12. I enjoy deadheading the spent flowers, but this is not necessary. If you do deadhead, use sharp, pointed scissors and be careful not to break off the buds that appear farther down the stem.

13. When all the flowering is finished, your iris bed will appear tidier if you cut down the flower stalks and leave the foliage to stand alone.

14. After about three years, your iris rhizomes can be divided and shared. After flowering, simply pluck the rhizomes from the soil and cut them into sections so that each piece has a foliage fan. Use a sharp, alcohol-cleaned knife for cutting. Replant part and give part away. Dividing irises is a no-brainer and actually makes them bloom better, so sharing is painless.

EMBELLISHING YOUR IRIS INTERLUDE

My iris bed has only irises in it, but I have seen combination iris and peony beds. Since both plants enjoy the same conditions, simply intermingle roots. The iris foliage will hide the fading peony foliage, and since peony leaves stand up off the ground on stalks, the foliage will allow light and air to reach the iris rhizomes. Peonies are tough old boots, too, and will thrive in the same neglect showered upon your iris.

You may also sow annual poppies into the soil between iris rhizomes. These delicate plants like poor, dry soil and leave sweet little seed heads when the bloom time is over. Annual poppies reseed freely, but the vibrant-colored Shirley types will eventually revert to duller colors. To sow poppies, scatter seeds over the bed as early in spring as possible. Some gardeners sow poppies on top of snow.

TWENTY-NINE

Fashion A Sunflower Folly

WHAT'S THE PAYOFF?

This large project shows you how to transform a dull part of your property into a folly bursting with a thousand sunflowers. Traditionally, a garden folly is a whimsical structure characterized by over-the-top eccentricity. Sometimes a folly will take the form of a monk's hideaway, a small-scale castle, or a nonsensical Asian temple. Clearly, a real garden folly takes a bit of cashola to construct, but every garden should have a touch of nuttiness and this sunflower folly delivers quirkiness on a budget.

Big, clown-like sunflowers are amusing enough in themselves, but imagine having a thousand blooms bursting from a 35 x 35 bed. My own sunflower folly was that size and boasted twenty-two different varieties. It was a crowd-pleaser, for sure, and cost only twenty-two packets of seeds to make.

If you don't have the time, space, or desire to make such a large folly, you can easily downscale this project. Simply adjust the dimensions and

TRIED-AND-TRUE SUNFLOWER TYPES

Most sunflower seed packets contain fifty seeds. Fifty seeds times twenty-two varieties equals 1,100 plantings—enough that a few dud seeds won't mess up your thousand-plant goal. Here are the types I used, ranging in height between 1½ feet to over 7 feet tall, and shining in golds and yellows, plus reds, oranges, maroons, and near-whites.

'Piccolo'	'Inca Jewels'	'Luna'	'Orange Sun'
'Zebulon'	'Sunspot'	'Teddy Bear'	'Hallo'
'Mammoth Russian'	'Italian White'	'Japanese Silverleaf'	'Sunbeam'
'Sunrich Orange'	'Evening Sun'	'Music Box'	'Large-Flowered Mix'
'Sunrich Lemon'	'Sunburst'	'Sunrise'	'Valentine'
'Sunset'		'Lemon Queen'	

contents of your folly accordingly. For example, if you have the perfect spot but it is 10 x 10, go with seven different varieties. Just be sure to devote as much space as possible to ensure that your folly is jolly.

Before you begin this project, you will need to have a fresh new flower bed as per the instructions in "Make a New Bed," page 15. I also found that a deer fence was essential and, in fact, my sunflower folly was the first area that I enclosed on my property. See page 69 for "Install a Deer Fence."

Because a folly is, by definition, eccentric, you can place it wherever you like. Mine was positioned on a boring dry slope of lawn that I tired of mowing. You can also use this folly to block out the road or screen your patio from the neighbors. A great sunflower folly will not only attract human attention (mine ended up in "Talk of the Town" in *The New Yorker*) but will also bring many different types of seed-eating birds (goldfinches, cardinals, and chickadees) into your garden. *(See "Attract Birds" on page 64.)*

You need not worry about coddling your sunflower folly. These fast-growing annuals like poor, rocky soil just fine and, once they get going, they require very little water. I did not bother to weed my folly because those sunflowers bolted up so fast that the few weeds that popped up were soon shadowed out. During wet summers, sunflowers sometimes get mildew on their leaves, but this is of no concern because it does not affect the production of flowers. Do not spray your sunflowers, as this will keep birds from winging in and decorating your creation.

Planting sunflowers is so easy that even little kids can help until their attention spans run out. As these annuals are big heat lovers, you simply must refrain from planting too early. In Zone 5 where I live, sunflowers are not planted before June 1 and will still tower over six feet tall by mid-August. These babies shoot skyward, so don't lean over the seedlings to look or you might get your eye poked out.

PURCHASE PRIOR TO INSTALLATION

- Sunflower seed packets (22 packets to fill 35 square feet *or* 7 packets to fill 10 square feet, etc. You do the math.)
- Reemay floating row cover: enough to cover entire area with extra cloth around edges
- Clothesline rope: white, 3 or 4 sections, each 6 feet long
- Clothespins

TOOLS

- Trowel

INSTALLATION

NOTE: *Your folly bed should be clean and bare as per the instructions for "Make a New Bed" on page 15. You may erect the deer fence either before or after planting your seeds.*

1. Begin in one corner of your bed and drape the piece of clothesline in a small, roughly pie-slice-shaped swath to show where you'll plant the seeds from your first packet. The shortest sunflowers (mine were 'Teddy Bear') go here.

2. With a trowel, plant the seeds about 6 inches apart and about 1 inch

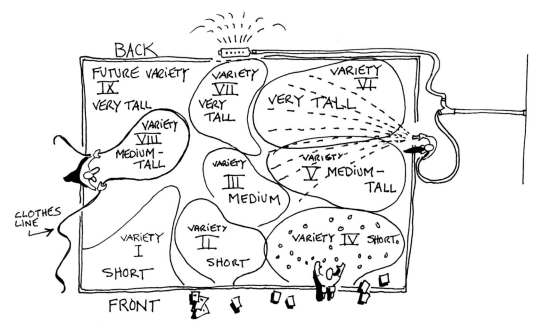

deep. Pat the soil hard with your hand to give the seed a firm foot-
ing. Continue until all seeds in this packet are planted.

3. Write the location of this variety on the packet and start a small
   map. Keep packets and map for your garden records.

4. Take the next section of clothesline and drape it on the ground in a
   wave shape adjacent to the first planted section. The object of all
   this draping and swathing is to prevent straight rows of sunflowers.
   This folly should undulate with waves of color.

5. Plant next shortest sunflowers here. (Mine was 'Zebulon'.) In your
   mind's eye, imagine that the complete bed will have the tallest flowers in the center of the folly, so that every shining face will be visible.

6. Plant seeds as per instructions in steps 2 and 3.

7. Start planting the third packet by arranging a short wave with the
   third piece of clothesline. As you move out from your first corner,
   you can lift and reuse that first piece of clothesline as needed. Plant
   seeds until you are all tuckered out for the day.

8. Cover the planted area with Reemay floating row cover weighed down with stones. If you neglect to do this, the crows will eat your work at dawn.

9. Continue planting, patting, and swathing until all your seeds are in. Then plant a kiss upon your helper and pat yourself on the back.

10. Water the planted area (about 1 inch deep, measured in a tin can set in the bed).

11. With the bed entirely planted, rearrange all row cover as follows: Lift Reemay above soil surface by positioning logs, bricks, or overturned flowerpots underneath the material. Use clothespins to attach long strips of fabric together and weigh down outer edges with stones, bricks, or heavy logs. It doesn't matter if the Reemay droops a bit onto the planted soil. The idea here is to make some "give" so that the seeds can sprout upward.

12. Sunflowers are annuals that sprout quickly when the soil has been warmed. You should see some under-the-covers action within one week.

13. When the sprouts are about 3 inches tall, you can remove the Reemay entirely. It doesn't matter if some of the more enthusiastic seedlings are a bit hunched over—they will straighten up pronto.

14. Although the seeds themselves attract flocks of gobbling crows, once they have germinated, the greedy birds are not interested. You must, however, have your deer fence in before you expose this "gourmet tender field greens salad" to those four-legged foragers.

15. As your sunflowers grow, you may water the folly during prolonged dry periods. You may also weed between the plants if you like. I did not because sunflowers are such aggressive growers that weeds are quickly shadowed out.

SUNFLOWER ARRANGING

Because they tend to have very heavy heads, sunflowers usually end up looking downward when cut for arranging. You might want to pick the smaller-flowered sunflowers for arranging ('Hallo'), or you can plan to set your vase high up on a mantel or armoire. Since sunflowers tend to be top-heavy, I use very large vases that have a bottom layer of stones for ballast.

A beautiful way to display your largest sunflowers is to cut the stem off right at the head and set the flower, face-up, in a large shallow bowl. You can also skip the bowl and just allow the flowers to dry naturally on the table.

CELEBRATE YOUR SUNFLOWERS

Because it is easy for the word about your folly to get around town, expect a few phone calls. A class of local third graders visited to have a math lesson among the towering sunflowers. They studied measuring and comparisons and were cute as the dickens.

We also had a grown-up cocktail party and let everyone wander around through the tall stalks. Even investment banker types said that they felt like kids again, but we did not break out the math books on that occasion.

16. My sunflower folly (planted the first week of June) was in full, brake-screeching glory by mid-August. Seeds begin to ripen by the end of August, by which time the goldfinches begin visiting, kissing and courting in the folly like reckless starlets at a Hollywood party. Have a sunflower party now.

17. Leave your sunflowers to stand proud all winter. When it's time to replant, pull up the stalks and put in your long-working compost pile. Chipping first will make them break down faster.

IV.

KEEP GROWING: ADD EDIBLES IN INCREMENTS

I love to eat and, thankfully, I love to cook, so it has never been a stretch for me to grow good food in my garden. When I was just getting started, I grew the usual suspects—easy salad greens, juicy tomatoes, and handfuls of herbs—and enjoyed every morsel. Even though I expected my homegrown produce to be better than what I could buy in the store, what surprised me every season was how *far much better* homegrown was than store-bought. Honestly, when I learned how crunchy and tasty lettuce could really be, how warm and lively tomatoes could taste, and how heady herbs should be, well, there was no way that I was not going to expand my food-growing efforts.

As you read through these projects, you might wonder, "Hmmm, is a homegrown onion really superior to a store-purchased onion?" Or you might say, "There is no way that I am going to grow cabbage." But, I am here to tell you that until you have sautéed a just-picked onion or cut into a cabbage so fresh and crisp that it actually has torque, you have no idea of the incredible taste potential of even the humblest edibles. I truly believe that growing our food made me a far better cook and has made all of us healthy, happy eaters. You don't have to grow everything you eat, but if you just try to grow something to eat, I guarantee you'll never have better.

I always tell people that you don't have to plow up the back forty to raise a little food for your table. As our family expanded with children, and then got smaller as they flew the nest, my vegetable garden has been bigger and smaller. Also, in years when I was on book tour for the entire summer, there was no vegetable garden at all. Then again, as I prepared to write a vegetable cookbook, it got bigger again and, voilà!, we entertained a lot. So, don't ever feel that your vegetable garden is a static responsibility because, perhaps even more so than the ornamental garden, a vegetable garden can change in size and scope every year just as your little heart (and tummy) desires.

Since it's always best to start small, the seven projects in this section show you how to create a beginner's salad garden that can be logically expanded to include the gourmet treats you have always wanted. You can follow in order, or pick and choose as you desire: It's your garden!

The first three projects explain how to grow the most popular edibles.

This project is a blueprint showing how to expand your salad garden and increase your vegetable harvest.

These three projects explain how to grow gourmet vegetables within the expanded potager blueprinted above.

THIRTY

PICK YOUR OWN SALAD

WHAT'S THE PAYOFF?

This large project shows you how to lay out and plant a salad garden to feed two people and their weekend guests. There's no quicker way to stake an emotional claim to your land than to grow a bit of food for your table. This project is a manageable start, yielding a salad garden that can be gradually expanded in future seasons to include many other vegetables. Honestly, the trick with growing food is to avoid the temptation to grow bushels of seventy different things. The joy you will get from this simple salad patch will be that you're going to make it small and keep it simple.

The key to a great little salad garden is sunshine. To find out what part of your property receives maximum light, use four stakes to mark the corners of a potential 20 x 20-foot patch. (These are my recommended dimensions, but of course, you may customize your space as you like.) To ascertain sun exposure, note how long the pretend square remains sunny each day. Observe it over several days' time at different periods of the day. Sometimes nudging the patch a few feet to the east or south can make a huge difference in capturing sunlight.

Once you have chosen your sunny location, I recommend clearing the entire 20 x 20 square feet of lawn and weeds using the Savvy Way Method for "Make a New Bed" on page 15. Taking time to clear the area like this gets your salad patch off to a weed-free start.

I also recommend that you grow salads and vegetables in raised beds as per the instructions below. Raised beds allow the soil to warm more quickly in spring, they allow for foot traffic without compression of the soil in the beds, they make planting and weeding very simple, and raised beds just look so endearingly domestic.

The plan outlined below allows for four raised beds, with a logical way to expand later to allow for the addition of cooking vegetables, perennial treats, root vegetables, and an asparagus patch. If you expand your salad garden with vegetables for cooking, you will have a potager (po-ta-ZHAY), French for kitchen garden. (Instructions for expanding this salad garden are found in "Manage Your Potager" on page 229. The rest of the edibles mentioned here have their own projects, too.)

If you live in an area with a big deer population, you must protect your salad garden as per "Install a Deer Fence" on page 69. My first salad garden, which grew into a larger vegetable potager, still has its original, expanded deer fence, so this is an investment that lasts.

Once installed, your raised-bed salad patch does not require much work beyond watering *(see "Water Wisely," page 57),* watching for bugs *(see "Don't Get Bugged," page 51),* and the odd bit of weeding *(See "Stay on Top of Weeds," page 44).* Harvest your salad as per the instructions on your seed packets and nursery tags, remembering that constant picking will keep production levels high. *(See "How to Pick Your Own Salad," page 213, for harvest and storage tips. I've also included my favorite salad dressing recipe.)*

PURCHASE PRIOR TO INSTALLATION

- Weed barrier cloth: for path areas as described below
- Inexpensive mulch to cover the weed barrier: wood chips, hay, pine bark
- 2 x 10 untreated lumber: 8 pieces to make 4 raised beds (Note: It is important to use untreated lumber or non-rotting cedar in vegetable gardens. Treated lumber contains arsenic that leaches into the soil with time.)
- Compost (if you don't have your own) to add to boxes
- Topsoil: 4 big bags
- Seeds: 4 packets total, select for leaf lettuce, arugula, spinach, mache, lamb's quarters, mustard, or mesclun
  or Nursery 6 packs: 2 each of 4 selected above (12 plants each)
- Seeds: radishes and carrots, 1 packet each
- Cucumber: small bush type, seeds or nursery 6-pack
- Tomato plants: 3 or 6 as per "Take Time for Tomatoes," page 217
- Nasturtium seeds: 1 packet
- Marigolds: nursery 6-packs, 2 for 12 plants total
- OPTIONAL: Mailbox for storing inexpensive scissors, hand cultivator, trowel, and other tools that will stay at the salad garden for convenience. An extra harvest basket stored at the salad garden also comes in handy.

TOOLS

- Saw for cutting lumber into 5-foot lengths (or have wood cut at lumber yard)
- Hammer and nails for making boxes for raised beds
- Garden rake
- Trowel
- Planter markers and indelible-ink pen
- Floating row cover

INSTALLATION

1. Begin with an area 20 x 20 feet that is clear of weeds and lawn (as explained in "Make a New Bed," page 15).

2. Using lumber cut to size, construct four squares that measure 5 x 5 feet. These will become raised beds. (If your arms are too short to reach to the middle of a 5 x 5 square, adjust accordingly.)

3. For paths: Position squares within the cleared area so that you have a pair of perpendicular, 4-foot-wide paths in between the beds. This should leave a 3-foot-wide path around the entire perimeter.

4. Cover pathways with weed barrier cloth cut to fit. You will need two 4 x 20-foot pieces for the two intersecting paths between the beds. You will also need four 3 x 20 pieces for the perimeter paths.

5. Disguise weed barrier cloth with chosen mulch. Paths are complete.

6. For beds: Dump one bag of topsoil into each bed. It is not crucial to fill each box to the top, as you will add compost every year.

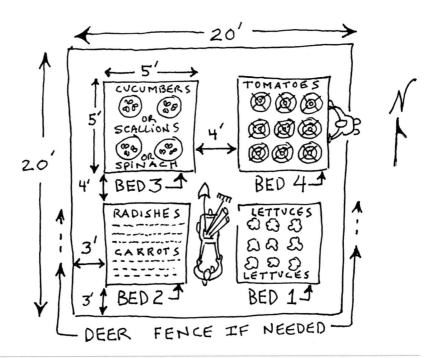

7. Smooth with a garden rake.
8. Add as much compost as you have to each bed and rake smooth. You do not have to dig this in.
9. Pat soil inside boxes firmly with your hand. It should not be too fluffy or too hard, just firm. This allows seeds and roots to take hold.
10. You now have four beds ready to plant. Below is a suggested planting scheme that may be amended to suit your tastes.
11. Bed one (southeast bed): Greens. Plant short plants like lettuces here. If planting seeds, follow packet instructions, mark with plant markers, and cover with floating row cover to aid germination. Otherwise, transplant seedlings as per nursery instructions.
12. Save all seed packets and nursery tags for your garden records.
13. Bed two (southwest bed): Radishes and carrots. Plant seeds as per packet instructions. Mark with plant markers and cover with floating row cover to aid germination. Radishes and carrots are not available as seedlings and must be grown from seeds.
14. Bed three (northwest bed): Cucumbers. Plant seeds as per packet instructions, mark and cover as steps above. Or transplant seedlings as per nursery instructions.
15. Bed four (northeast bed): Tomatoes. Transplant and grow as per complete instructions in "Take Time for Tomatoes," page 217. This bed allows for three tomato plants.
16. Please note: If you do not like cucumbers, substitute another bed of tomatoes, or a bed of scallions

HOW TO PICK YOUR OWN SALAD

- Harvest salad regularly in early morning when plants are at their crispest stage.
- Use scissors to clip leaves of baby lettuces, arugula, and other greens. Push soil away from top shoulders of radishes and carrots to check for desired size before pulling.
- Cukes are sweeter and crispier when smaller.
- Pick tomatoes when totally ripe and not one day before.
- Wash all harvest in sink.
- Rinse fresh greens, dry in spinner, loosely roll in paper towels, place inside plastic bags, and keep in the crisper. Ditto radishes and carrots.
- Cukes go unwashed in paper bags in the crisper. Wash only moments before using to prevent soft spots.
- Store tomatoes outside of the fridge.

and spinach, or another bed of lettuces. The plan above allows the maximum amount of sun to fall on the plants.

17. When all beds are planted with salad material, squeeze in marigold seedlings and nasturtium seeds. These traditional plants steer bugs away from your edibles. Nasturtium flowers and leaves can be eaten, marigolds cannot.

18. This salad garden should be watered at least 1 inch early the next morning. Thereafter, it should receive 1 inch of water per week.

19. OPTIONAL: Erect deer fence if needed. *(See "Install a Deer Fence," page 69.)*

20. OPTIONAL: In a metal mailbox, store inexpensive scissors, hand cultivator, etc., for quick work in salad patch. This is also a good place to store cloth strips for tying up tomato plants and, on top, an extra harvest basket.

Katherine's Favorite Fresh Garden Salad

Tossed with a garlicky dressing made right in the bowl, this salad is a virtual garden explosion of fresh flavor. Note that the quantities of vegetables, herbs, and greens are flexible; use whatever you have popping out of your garden, and the result will be delicious.

1 GARLIC CLOVE, HALVED

2 TABLESPOONS EXTRA-VIRGIN OLIVE OIL

$^1/_8$ TEASPOON DRY MUSTARD

$^1/_8$ TEASPOON SWEET PAPRIKA

$^1/_8$ TEASPOON FRESHLY GROUND BLACK PEPPER

FRESH GARDEN HERBS

FRESH ONIONS OR SCALLIONS

FRESH CARROTS

FRESH RADISHES

FRESH CUCUMBERS

FRESH TOMATOES

FRESH GREENS

CIDER VINEGAR OR LEMON JUICE

Rub the cut garlic along the inside of a large, wooden salad bowl.

Pour the olive oil into the bowl and add the mustard, paprika, and pepper. Blend well to emulsify.

Snip fresh herbs with scissors, and add to the oil. Slice onions or scallions into thin pieces and add to the bowl, tossing gently.

Slice carrots, radishes, cukes, and tomatoes into bite-sized chunks, place in bowl on top of oil mixture, but do not stir.

Shred fresh greens by hand and place on top of the vegetables, but do not stir. Refrigerate bowl until ready to serve, but no longer than 2 hours.

Immediately prior to serving, toss salad ingredients so that the oil mixture coats everything. Add a drizzle of cider vinegar or lemon juice and toss again. Taste and add more vinegar or lemon juice as desired.

Salad fixin's

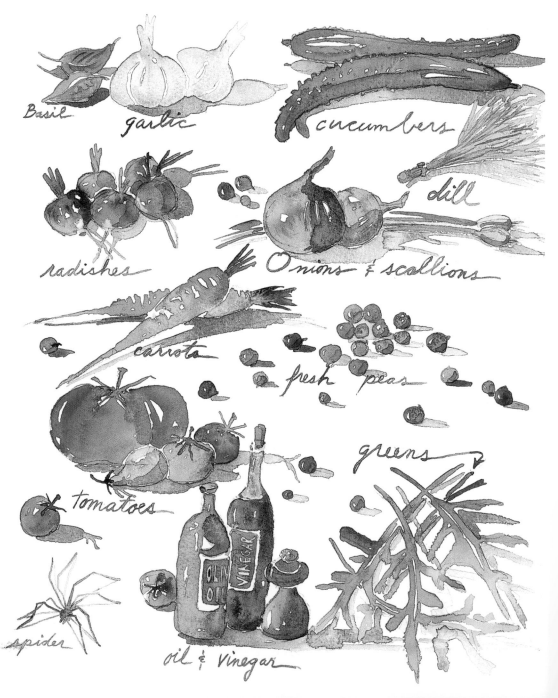

Basil

garlic

cucumbers

dill

radishes

Onions & scallions

carrots

fresh peas

tomatoes

greens

spider

oil & vinegar

WHAT'S THE PAYOFF?

This small project shows you how to grow the tastiest tomatoes you've ever had. Homegrown tomatoes are probably the most popular edible in American gardens. Although some lesser-evolved gardeners aim to have the first red tomato on the block, this silly type of contest involves lots of ugly accoutrement and rarely produces the delicious, juicy delicacy that a gourmet gardener craves. Good food cannot be rushed and a great tomato takes time.

I recommend buying small tomato plants over starting your own seeds indoors. Any nursery now offers a large selection of heirloom and hybrid tomatoes at very reasonable prices. Purchase small plants (nursery packs are fine) and avoid the temptation to buy those that have already bloomed. Bigger tomato plants have bigger setbacks when transplanted into your garden.

I try to grow three different tomato types: slicers, cookers, and tidbits. Slicers are the large, juicy tomatoes that make a hamburger right

Slicers:
- Cherokee Purple
- Big Rainbow
- Persimmon
- Brandywine

Cookers:
- Amish Paste
- Super Sarno
- La Rossa
- Principe Borghese

Tidbits:
- Sungold
- Sweet One Hundred
- Red or Yellow Currant

off the grill a gourmet treat. Cookers are for making rich sauces and are smaller, slightly football-shaped, and less juicy. Tidbit tomatoes are the little guys that come in various small shapes perfect for popping whole into your mouth. Tailor your selection to fit your desires and family size. For our family of four, I plant two or three plants of each type, varying my selection each year.

Tomato plants are divided into determinate and indeterminate plant forms. This concerns you because a determinate tomato plant ripens all its fruit at about the same time. This is fantastic if you are planning to can a lot of tomato sauce. Determinate tomato plants are bushy (topping out at around three to four feet), work well in containers, need no pinching out, and don't usually need staking. An indeterminate tomato plant ripens its fruit over the entire growing season, stopping only when frost hits. Indeterminate tomatoes are actually vines (reaching six feet tall and more), they require more space vertically, you need to pinch off side shoots, and they require staking. Even though I am pretty lazy, I grow indeterminate tomatoes because this group includes the heirlooms, and to me, the extra effort is more than paid off by superior taste.

The first requirement for growing superior tomatoes is sun. A good tomato plant requires eight hours of sun to be productive. Your salad garden probably offers this, and that is the perfect place to plant these sun lovers. I have seen people with otherwise shady gardens who save their sunniest spots for growing tomatoes. There is a family in my village that parks their BMW in the street for the entire summer to make room for spackle buckets of tomato plants in their sunny driveway. These people have their priorities right.

The next most important consideration in growing great tomatoes is heat. Do not rush to transplant your baby tomato plants into a still-chilly garden. Think of tomatoes like any other tropical plants: Unless the nighttime temperatures have steadily remained above 45 degrees, the plant is going to suffer and be prone to bugs and diseases. In my Zone 5 garden, I wait until after Memorial Day to transplant tomatoes into the garden.

The third trick to growing great tomatoes is a little surprising: A great tomato does not come from an overfertilized, overwatered plant. Do not put manure or any high-nitrogen fertilizer in your tomato beds. This produces lots of leaves but fruit that is too soft and prone to rot. *(See "Fertilize Effectively," page 38.)*

Do not pick tomatoes until they are fully ripe. Wait until the fruit feels heavy and almost falls into your hand. Your first homegrown tomato should be consumed on the spot while it is still as warm as a freshly laid egg, while it still smells like the garden, and with its juices running down your arm. It'll definitely be worth the wait.

PURCHASE PRIOR TO INSTALLATION

- Tomato plants: 2 or 3 of each as per information above
- Tomato cages: 1 for each determinate plant
- Sturdy garden stakes: 7 feet tall, one for each indeterminate plant
- Compost (if you don't have your own)

TOOLS

- Shovel or trowel
- Aluminum foil
- Garden twine
- Old sheets or soft rags ripped into strips for later tying up

INSTALLATION

1. Plot tomato plant positions in clean, weed-free bed. Allow about 20 inches between determinate plants and 30 inches between indeter-

minate plants. If these will be planted in your salad garden, make sure that taller tomato plants do not shade out other shorter vegetables. (In the plan on page 232, tomatoes are planted in bed 4, a northeast bed.)

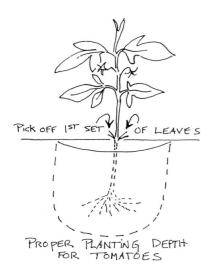

Pick off 1st set OF LEAVES

PROPER PLANTING DEPTH FOR TOMATOES

2. Prepare plants by removing any yellow leaves, any blossoms, and any small fruit.

3. Water plants thoroughly and allow it to soak in before removing them from nursery pack or container.

4. All tomato plants: Transplant tomatoes deeply, up to their first set of leaves. Tomato plants are exceptions to the usual rule "transplant at same soil depth as when potted." Tomatoes are planted deeply because the buried stem produces more roots sideways, stabilizing the plant and allowing it to absorb more nutrients.

5. If determinate: Dig a hole with the trowel. Add a scoop of your compost. Transplant deeply as above.

6. Place sturdy tomato cage over determinate plant and firmly push into soil.

7. If indeterminate: Position wooden stakes before transplanting. Fashion teepee arrangement with three stakes tied together at top. The bottom end of each stake should be buried about 1 foot deep or stabilized with stones. Plants will become heavy with fruit and prone to tipping over.

8. Dig a hole, add a scoop of compost, and transplant deeply as per step 4, positioning one plant next to each stake.

9. For all tomato plants: Use the aluminum foil to make a ring around the stem of each plant on the surface of the soil. This will help to deter cutworms.

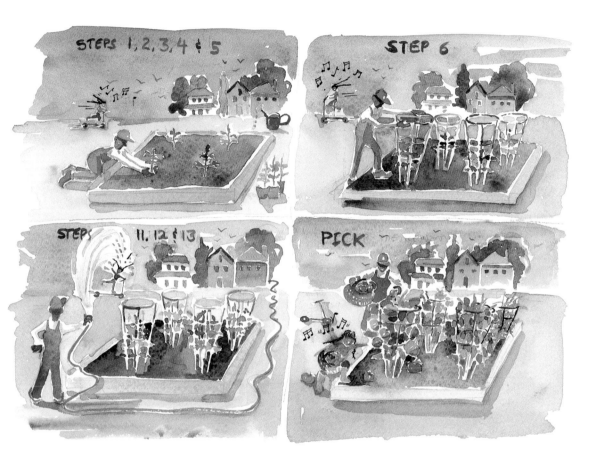

10. Place old sheets (or any soft material) ripped into strips nearby for constant tying up as plants grow. Keeping plants off the ground helps prevent diseases.

11. If possible, water plants at base, not overhead. This also prevents diseases.

12. Fertilize sparingly and stop altogether once small fruits appear.

13. Water sparingly once fruits appear. Too much watering (or rain) causes split tomatoes.

14. Once the ground has thoroughly warmed (end of June here), mulch

around the base of plants. This prevents soil splashes that promote disease.

15. Handpick bugs and drop them into jar of soapy water. *(See "Don't Get Bugged," page 51.)*

COMPANION PLANTING WITH TOMATOES

Companion planting is a fascinating facet of traditional organic gardening. Through trial and error over many years, experienced gardeners discovered that certain plants thrived in close proximity to other plants, some plants helped repel diseases and pests that preyed upon other plants, and, finally, some plants actually fared worse when planted near each other.

Each plant in the booklet Companion Planting and Intensive Cultivation *(Rodale Press, 1981) has a long list of friends and enemies, but since we are talking tomatoes here, have a look at the almost-magical ways you can influence your tomato yield.*

Tomatoes thrive in proximity to asparagus, cucumbers, onions, and peppers. Keep tomato pests and diseases at bay with basil, chives, marigolds, and mint. Tomatoes can be weakened by shared diseases when planted near potatoes and corn. Finally, and most strangely, tomatoes planted near mature dill plants or kohlrabi will exhibit stunted growth.

THIRTY-TWO

HAVE SOME HERBS

WHAT'S THE PAYOFF?

This small project shows you how to plan and plant an herb patch. Culinary herbs are simple to grow. They prefer a dry sunny spot and will taste far better if you forgo all fertilizing and most watering. This means that it is better to make a separate bed of herbs than to add these tasty toughies to your salad garden or flower beds. Rich soil and regular watering take the tang out of homegrown herbs.

Culinary herbs are cheap and cheerful edibles that garner tons of respect even though their cultivation is nearly effortless. Salads, meats, and brewed teas get a taste kick when herbs are tossed at them. But even if your idea of cooking is nuking a pizza, scattering that frozen Frisbee with homegrown herbs will take you into a whole new world of delight.

Obtaining herb plants is simple. Ten years ago, culinary herbs were available only in limited variety at nurseries. Now, even the Home-Mega-Store offers scores and scores of herbs in nursery pots or nursery six-packs. I prefer to purchase herb plants rather than to grow them from seed. Many herb seeds are difficult to germinate and the price of seed packets soon approaches the price of inexpensive plants.

This herb project begins with a south-facing bed in a dry sunny spot ready for planting. *(See "Make a New Bed," page 15.)* Allow at least one square foot per herb, because you want to have enough herbs to really be useful. It is too stingy to add one or two leaves to the salad. Grow handfuls of herbs: You will always be able to use or give away extras.

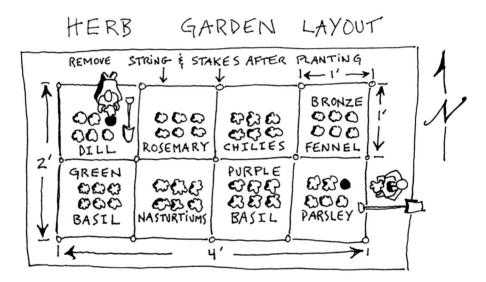

A brand-new gardener might want to plan an herb patch two feet wide and four feet long with space for eight different culinary herbs. Twelve different herbs can be grown in a bed three feet wide and four feet long. It's always a good idea to start on the small side and, if you find you'd like to increase the size, see the end of the instructions for a design suggestion. Most gardeners like to grow herbs near the kitchen door, as this makes harvesting quick and simple.

All you readers out there in warmer areas, please don't laugh too loudly when I say that rosemary should be treated like an annual. I adore those rosemary hedges in Southern California and will trade a FedEx box of sweet spring tulip flowers for your fresh hedge trimmings any day!

OREGANO	perennial; spreads by runners, so be careful; try golden also; leaves and flowers edible
THAI BASIL	annual; smaller and much tastier leaf than Italian basil; leaves and flowers edible
THYME	perennial; creeping thyme is hard to harvest; culinary type is a little bush; leaves and flowers edible
SAGE	perennial; make sure it's a culinary type; try tricolor or variegated; leaves and flowers edible
CHIVES	perennial; leaves and flowers edible
FLAT PARSLEY	biennial; flat leaves are nicer than frizzy ones; edible leaves
LEMON BALM	perennial; great for tea; edible leaves and flowers
CHILES	annual; harvest fruits with gloves and avoid eye and nose contact
ROSEMARY	in cold areas, treat as annual; cut tender sprouts; leaves and flowers edible
BAY	treat as annual (as above) or bring inside; harvest whole leaves as needed for flavoring
BRONZE FENNEL	treat as annual; all parts edible
DILL	annual; foliage, flowers, pollen, and seeds edible
PURPLE BASIL	small-leaved has best taste (beautiful on yellow tomatoes)
CILANTRO	annual; all parts edible; this one is easy to grow from seeds
LEMONGRASS	treat as annual; use leaves like bay for flavoring
NASTURTIUMS	annual; flowers edible; easy to grow from seeds
GARLIC CHIVES	perennial; leaves and flower buds edible
BURNET	annual; cucumber-tasting leaves edible
LOVAGE	perennial; celery-tasting leaves edible
MARJORAM	perennial; leaves and flowers edible
MINT	Mint likes a moist, slightly shaded location and tends to spread by underground runners. For these reasons, keep mint out of your herb patch.

PURCHASE PRIOR TO INSTALLATION

- Herb plants: 6 small plants of each, 1 herb type per 1 square foot of patch
- Builder's sand: 1 bag, to amend wet soil (do not buy if you have quick-draining, sandy soil)

TOOLS

- Trowel
- Garden stakes and string
- Plant markers and indelible-ink pen

INSTALLATION

1. Prepare a new bed bare of weeds and lawn as per Savvy Way in "Make a New Bed," page 15. Herb patch must be in full sun. Allow 1 square foot per herb type.
2. If soil drainage is poor, pour sand on top of bed and work into top several inches of soil with trowel. It is not necessary to dig in deeply, as herbs are shallow rooted.
3. Use garden stakes and string to divide the bed into 1-foot squares. For example, divide a 2 x 4-foot bed into 8 squares.
4. Position tallest herbs at rear of south-facing bed to avoid shading shorter herbs in front.
5. If necessary, draw a map of the bed to remind yourself which herbs are planted where. Save this map and all nursery tags for your garden records.
6. Remove herbs from packs or pots and plant them in the patch at the same soil level. Planting too deeply will cause rot and too shallowly will cause roots to desiccate. Firm with your fingers soil around the plant so that roots can grasp the soil.
7. Plant 6 herbs of the same kind in 1 square. This will produce a full herb bed in a season and will appear more ornamental than the dotted look. Plant herbs closer to middle of square rather than around the edges. This will help delineate different herbs.

OTHER HERBS

There are herbs that I grow outside my culinary beds that we do not eat. I do not recommend self-dosing with medicinal herbs.

LAVENDER	*perennial; I don't like the taste, but I do like the fragrance; dry as described above and use in bathwater and in dresser drawers*
COMFREY	*perennial; use fresh leaves steeped in a bucket of water to make natural plant fertilizer (See "Fertilize Effectively," page 38.)*
BORAGE	*annual; beautiful butterfly magnet, but too fuzzy for my taste*
CLARY SAGE	*biennial; beautiful but also really fuzzy*
ECHINACEA	*perennial; beautiful flowers in borders; dangerous for dogs*
CATNIP	*life span depends upon morals of your cat*
VALERIAN	*perennial; very pretty in borders*
PURSLANE	*I will warn you against this one, described in* Wyman's Gardening Encyclopedia *as "probably the worst weed troubling all gardeners throughout the U.S. and Canada." I planted it once and regret it forever.*

8. Use plant markers for each square. This will allow you to send guests out to the patch to pick herbs while you are busy cooking.
9. Remove stakes and string when finished planting.
10. Place a rain gauge in the bed, and use a sprinkler until ½ inch of water is measured.
11. Do not put compost, manure, or any other fertilizer on the herb bed. Herbs are tastier when grown in poor soil.
12. Harvest herbs as needed. Sharp scissors work best. Clip tender tops of woody herbs like thyme and rosemary. Cut stems and foliage of soft-stemmed herbs like parsley, lovage, and burnet.

13. Before frost, harvest herbs and dry as described below.

14. To increase herb bed size for next year, apply the Savvy Way to "Make a New Bed" (page 15). If you already have a 2 x 4-foot herb patch, plan a matching patch with a 3-foot-wide grass strip in between. If your family's appetite for pesto or salsa is endless, allow more squares for basil or cilantro. Customize your herb beds as you do your flower garden.

EASY HERB DRYING

Although I adore cooking and eating food from my garden, canning and freezing produce just somehow never happens much anymore at my house. I have millions of excuses not to "put things up." Within the last few years I have wised up to my own slothful ways and devised a simple way to dry garden herbs for use year-round. You will be amazed at the superiority of your own homegrown, home-dried herbs. Their fragrance, texture, and taste will cause you to swear off store-bought herb dust-bunnies forever.

Dried herbs can be used for all cooking purposes, for brewing tea, and for adding to bathwater. (Place in cheesecloth or a reusable muslin bag tied with string to the faucet or prepare to call the plumber.) Extra dried herbs can be kept in a basket on the hearth and thrown into the flames to produce aromatic fires. (You can throw the unwanted stems in the fire anytime.)

All during the growing season, I harvest individual herbs (i.e., the basil or the rosemary or the parsley) and toss them, stems and all, into flat baskets for drying. I keep each type separate because, for example, rosemary dries quickly but parsley takes a while. You can also hang bunches of herbs upside-down to dry.

When the herb is entirely, absolutely crispy-crunchy dry, place it whole into a zipper-lock bag, squash out the air, and label it with a Sharpie. Store anywhere.

To use, squeeze zipped plastic bag carefully to crush contents. The herb leaves fall off the stems. Remove stems from the bag and discard. Use herbs as needed.

Manage Your Potager

WHAT'S THE PAYOFF?

I am going to give you fair warning: This project is not the stuff of great literary merit, but, rather, a hands-on blueprint how-to for growing a wide variety of the best vegetables you'll ever eat. People often say that the hardest part of making a vegetable garden is figuring out where to put everything they want to grow. This large project shows you how to create and manage a potager big enough to feed a family of four and their dinner guests for many months.

The garden described in "Pick Your Own Salad" *(page 209)* has four 5 x 5 beds (for a total area of 20 x 20, including ample paths) and is suitable for two people who want primarily fresh salad ingredients. This project for building a manageable potager yields a bigger kitchen garden. You will have room and a planting plan suitable for growing approximately seventeen different vegetables to be harvested over a long growing season. Once the potager is built, it remains in place for many, many years of delicious eating, so your return on the time invested is amply multiplied.

There will be great diagrams and instructions for organizing the large amount of information included here, so just trust me that this project is actually the quickest and easiest way to get a potager going today.

The potager described in this project doubles the number of salad-growing raised beds (each 5 x 5 feet) to eight beds. A plan for successive spring and summer plantings for the eight beds is included. This potager also includes two larger beds (14 x 3), one for a permanent asparagus bed *(see "Aspire to Asparagus," page 253)* and the other for potatoes, corn, and beans. The potager paths mirror those laid out in "Pick Your Own Salad," page 209, with the result that this project creates a garden with a perimeter of 40 x 26 feet to include ten beds total, each surrounded by ample paths.

You can go all the way to mega-vega garden heaven and create the entire potager in one fell swoop, or you can use the plan below and add beds and paths as several years progress. All beds here are created using the Savvy Way method on page 16 to make new beds. You know by now that I generally do not recommend rototilling to create a quick garden because your weed problems will be endless.

Refer to the garden plan on the following page. You'll see that the original raised salad beds are numbered 1–4 and the new raised beds are numbered 5–8. The permanent asparagus bed is bed 9, and another long bed for corn, beans, or potato plantings is bed 10.

You will need to purchase enough weed barrier cloth and mulch to completely clear potager addition A (20 x 20) and potager addition B (40 x 6) using the Savvy Way technique. When the turf is gone, you will recycle the weed barrier and mulch to a permanent position on the paths of the potager. Although this process might sound a bit involved at this stage, I promise I'll lead you step by step to the most productive potager you could ever imagine.

If you live in an area where deer roam, there is no point in making a potager unless you first enclose it with deer fencing. The way to make a deer fence is described fully in "Install a Deer Fence," page 69. Realistically, after you have achieved clean new beds via the Savvy Way, you should allow several weekends to fence and build your potager. Once again, this is the biggest project included in the book, but heck, who doesn't get enthusiastic about having great food?

You will see that there are many cross-references included in this project. Building this potager is an incremental process and involves other projects to greater or lesser degrees. However, I did not want to repeat information over and over and bore you to

tears. Here is an easy way to manage the information you need: Read the entire project and put small Post-its on the other pages that you need for reference. Take this book to your local copy shop and have all the marked pages copied. Also have this project photocopied. Insert the reference pages at their needed locations. Keep your marked copy of this project in your garden journal for future reference. *(See "Record Your Progress," page 32.)*

indelible markers

wooden plant markers

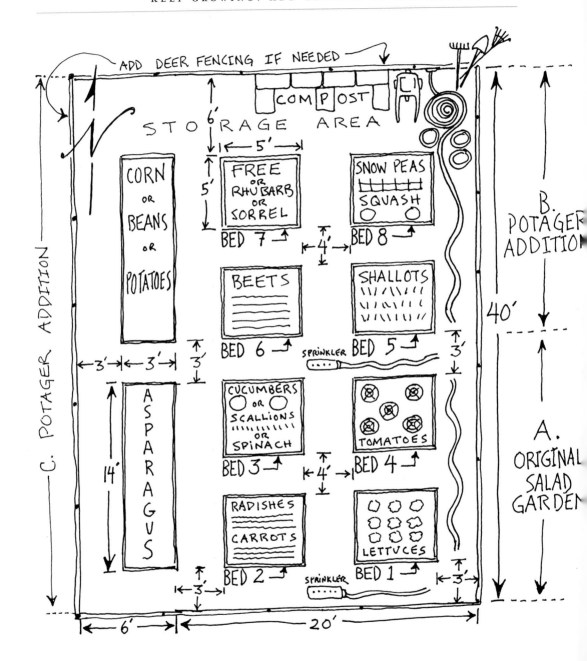

ADD DEER FENCING IF NEEDED

STORAGE AREA

COMPOST

CORN
OR
BEANS
OR
POTATOES

FREE
OR
RHUBARB
OR
SORREL
BED 7

SNOW PEAS
SQUASH
BED 8

BEETS
BED 6

SHALLOTS
BED 5

SPRINKLER

CUCUMBERS
OR
SCALLIONS
OR
SPINACH
BED 3

TOMATOES
BED 4

A
S
P
A
R
A
G
U
S

RADISHES
CARROTS
BED 2

LETTUCES
BED 1

SPRINKLER

B.
POTAGER
ADDITION

A.
ORIGINAL
SALAD
GARDEN

C. POTAGER ADDITION

6'

5'

5'

3'

3'

3'

3'

14'

4'

4'

3'

3'

40'

6'

20'

PURCHASE PRIOR TO INSTALLATION

- Woven weed barrier cloth: enough to cover 20 x 20 feet for addition A and enough to cover 14 x 6 feet for addition B
- Inexpensive mulch to cover weed barrier
- Deer fencing and posts to protect a complete 40 x 26-foot perimeter
- 2 x 10 untreated lumber, 8 pieces to make four raised beds (Note: The 14 x 3 beds are not raised and therefore do not require lumber edges.)
- Compost (if you don't have your own) to add to beds
- Topsoil: 4 big bags
- Seeds. Bed 1: lettuces and leeks (Bed plans are included to help you figure out what to put where. Feel free to substitute.)
- Seeds. Bed 2: radishes and carrots
- Seeds. Bed 3: scallions, spinach, and cucumbers
- Plants. Bed 4: tomatoes *(see "Take Time for Tomatoes," page 217)*
- Plants. Bed 5: shallot sets *(see "Root for Autumn Vegetables," page 237)*
- Plants. Bed 5: 2 pots of horseradish plants *(see "Add Perennial Edibles," page 247)*
- Seeds. Bed 6: beets *(see "Root for Autumn Vegetables," page 237)*
- Plants. Bed 6: 2 pots of rhubarb plants *(see "Add Perennial Edibles," page 247)*
- Seeds. Bed 7: seeds or plants of your favorite vegetable (okra, salsify, celery, kale, Brussels sprouts, kohlrabi, whatever)
- Plants. Bed 7: 2 pots of French sorrel *(see "Add Perennial Edibles," page 247)*
- Seeds. Bed 8: snow peas and squash
- Plants. Bed 9: asparagus crowns as per "Aspire to Asparagus," page 253
- Seeds. Bed 10: seed potatoes, corn, or beans

TOOLS

- Saw for cutting lumber into 5-foot lengths *or* have wood cut at lumber yard
- Hammer and nails for making boxes for raised beds
- Garden rake
- Trowel
- Shovel
- Plant markers and indelible-ink pen
- Floating row cover

INSTALLATION

1. Use Savvy Way method to clear entire area to become potager. *(See "Make a New Bed," page 15.)*
2. Erect a deer fence around entire perimeter as per "Install a Deer Fence," page 69.
3. To construct raised beds 5–8 and connecting paths: Follow steps 1–10 on page 212 in "Pick Your Own Salad." Allow a 6-foot-wide path at north end of the beds (as per diagram) for storage of pots, compost, hoses, sprinklers, extra tools, harvest baskets, etc. (If you do not already have a salad garden as per that project, construct beds 1–4 as above.)
4. To construct beds 9 and 10: These two beds are flush with the ground except for a slight elevation where compost is dumped on top as per planting directions.
5. Paths surrounding beds 9 and 10 are laid as per the diagram.
6. To manage bed 1: In early spring seed rows of lettuce as per instructions in "Pick Your Own Salad," page 209. When lettuces bolt, transplant baby leeks as per instructions on pages 238–39 in "Root for Autumn Vegetables."
7. To manage bed 2: Sow rows of radishes and carrots as per instructions in "Pick Your Own Salad," page 213. Successive sowings ensure continuous harvest.

8. To manage bed 3: Sow rows of scallions and spinach in early spring. When spinach bolts, sow 3 mounds of cukes as per packet. Scallions remain in bed with cukes and can be harvested all season.

9. To manage bed 4: This bed is for tomatoes. Plant as per "Take Time for Tomatoes," page 219. (Additional tomatoes can be grown in free space in bed 7.)

10. To manage bed 5: Transplant 2 horseradish plants in the north corners of the bed. These are perennial edibles as per page 250. Sow remaining space with shallot sets as per instructions in "Root for Autumn Vegetables," page 240.

11. To manage bed 6: Transplant 2 rhubarb plants in the north corners of the bed. These are perennial edibles as per page 250. Sow remaining space with beet seeds as per page 241, "Root for Autumn Vegetables."

12. To manage bed 7: Transplant 2 French sorrel plants to the north corners of the bed. These are perennial edibles as per page 249. Plant the remainder of the free space with vegetables of your choice.

13. To manage bed 8: Plant snow peas in very early spring as per packet instructions. When peas fade (about same time lettuce bolts), plant 3 hills of squash (yellow, zucchini, winter, delicata, acorn, or pumpkin). Allow vines to overrun bed into paths as summer progresses.

14. To manage bed 9: Plant asparagus crowns as described on page 256 in "Aspire to Asparagus." This is a long-lived perennial vegetable that can be harvested for ten years or more.

15. To manage bed 10: This bed has a 3-year rotation of pole beans, corn, and potatoes. This rotation promotes good harvests and discourages pests and diseases. Depending upon the year, purchase bean seeds, corn seeds, or seed potatoes and grow as per packet instructions.

16. To manage the potager in winter: Harvest late root crops before the ground freezes solidly. Leave kale and Brussels sprouts in place, as they will sweeten with frosts and continue to produce all winter.

17. Clear dead foliage and plant debris and place in the compost pile. Cover all beds with weed barrier and weigh down with stones to prevent weed growth.

18. To manage the potager in early spring: Remove weed barrier. Spread beds with compost and use the tonics as described in "Fertilize Effectively," page 38. Renew mulch on paths if necessary. Plant when ready!

THIRTY-FOUR

WHAT'S THE PAYOFF?

This small project explains how to extend your harvest season and keep your pantry stocked with garden produce all winter. The royal roots—leeks, shallots, carrots, and beets—can be tucked into the soil right in a small salad garden where bolted lettuces and spinach have been pulled up or they can be included in larger potager planning. Root vegetables are very easy to grow, they have low maintenance requirements, and they are the storable foodstuffs that put the zing of homegrown into all your cold-weather cooking. Try some and soon you'll be root-touting, too.

You might wonder why anyone would devote garden space to something like beets. Yes, for sure, just about everyone had a Wretched Root Vegetable Experience as a kid, usually involving some disaster of a dish that required hours of boiling. But I have a modern take on all these nutritious "keepers." I scrub them hard, leaving the skins intact, barely drizzle them with olive oil and sea salt, and cook or roast them until they're fork-tender. Because all these vegetables store perfectly without refrigeration, planting late vegetables in your potager allows you to keep a full pantry all winter.

If you planted squares of lettuces and spinach in your garden *(see "Pick Your Own Salad," page 209),* these will begin to bolt when your weather turns hot. Bolted greens, with the exception of arugula, do not taste nice at all, so you will be pulling these and leaving yourself with empty garden space perfect for a few autumn vegetables. Or, as mentioned earlier, you can follow the potager planting plan on page 232.

PURCHASE PRIOR TO INSTALLATION
- Leek seeds: 1 packet
- Seed flat: for germinating leeks
- Shallots: small bag of "sets" (sets are tiny shallot bulb-ettes)
- Carrot seeds: 1 packet
- Beet seeds: 1 packet
- Compost (if you don't have your own)

TOOLS
- Trowel
- Plant markers and indelible-ink pen
- Floating row cover

INSTALLATION
1. When your lettuces and spinach bolt, pull them and place in the compost pile.
2. Top-dress these previously planted areas with a thin layer of compost.
3. Leeks: For best results with leeks, plant seeds as early as April in seed flats. Keep baby leeks in flats watered.
4. To transplant little leeks: Water seed flat and wait a few minutes to soak in.

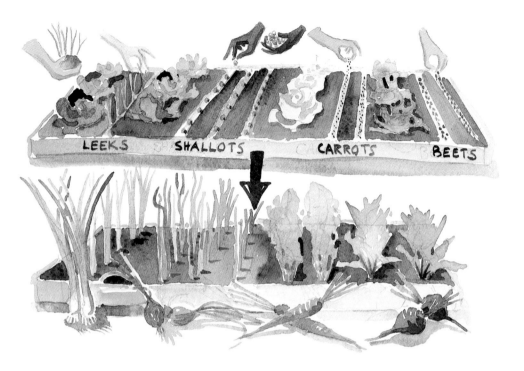

LEEKS   SHALLOTS   CARROTS   BEETS

5. Use a trowel to lever up a chunk of soil from the flat with the baby leeks and their roots intact.

6. Use the trowel to make a furrow for planting leeks. Pull the leeks apart with your fingers and space about 3 inches apart in the furrow. The furrow should be deep enough so that the leeks can be buried with just the top few inches of green showing. Water in before replacing soil in the furrow. This deep-planting technique precludes the need to hill up leeks.

7. Water well and cover the bed loosely with a floating row cover to speed growth.

8. Leeks taste best when they are less than 1 inch in diameter.

9. Leeks tolerate frost and freezing weather. To harvest, dig with a garden fork to avoid breaking.

10. Do not wash. Do not remove tops or roots. Let them dry in a warm

dry place until most of the soil shakes away. Store in brown paper bags in a cool pantry away from light. *(See page 242 for a recipe for Frizzled Leeks.)*

11. For shallots: In early spring, plant tiny shallot sets in between several rows of lettuce seed or follow the potager planting plan on page 232. (The shallots will continue to grow after the lettuces are removed.)

12. Mark rows of buried shallots with plant markers to avoid accidentally disturbing them.

13. To harvest shallots: Wait until green tops turn brown in autumn. Gently use a trowel to lever up clusters of bulbs. Do not wash soil off. Let them dry in a warm sunny place. Store covered with a dry kitchen towel in airy baskets in a cool dark place. (A recipe for Shallot S'mores follows.)

14. For carrots: After spinach and lettuces bolt, plant rows of carrots as per instructions on packet, or follow the potager planting plan on page 232. Mark rows with plant markers. Water well and cover soil with floating row cover.

15. Carrots are slow to germinate. Floating row cover and a gentle daily watering aid germination greatly.

16. Thin carrot seedlings as per instructions on packet. This is essential to good carrot crops. Put thread-like thinnings, including tiny green foliage, in salads.

17. Don't worry about carrots and frost. Carrots do not mind frost. October carrots are very sweet and delicious.

18. However, harvest all carrots before ground freezes solidly. Dig carefully with a garden fork to avoid breaking. Do not wash. Let the soil dry and crumble away. Store in brown paper bags in the pantry away from light and heat. (A recipe for Golden Carrot Soup is on page 244.)

19. For beets: Plant beet seeds in space where spinach and lettuces have bolted or follow the potager planting plan on page 232. Water well and cover with floating row cover. Beets are easy to germinate.

20. Thin beets according to packet directions. This step is key to a good beet harvest. Eat beet thinnings in salads.

21. Later in the growing season, check beet size by brushing soil away from the top of roots. Harvest beets when they're about 2 inches in diameter for best taste and texture.

22. Beets sweeten as the season cools. Harvest before the ground freezes solidly.

23. Use beet greens as you would spinach. Store unwashed beets as described for carrots in step 18. *(See page 245 for my Beet-O-Rama recipe.)*

hoses

Nozzles

connectors + valves

Frizzled Leeks

Leeks, mouthwatering members of the onion family, are not only delicious, but also among the healthiest vegetables I grow in my potager. Frizzled leeks are a snap to prepare, and are a scrumptious addition to steak (or chicken, or fish). Like onions, they reduce in volume considerably, so keep this in mind if you're cooking for a crowd.

6 MEDIUM TO LARGE LEEKS

2 TABLESPOONS EXTRA-VIRGIN OLIVE OIL

SEA SALT TO TASTE

Preheat the oven 350°F.

Wash leeks and dry them thoroughly.

Cut away the roots carefully to leave the root plate intact. Remove most of the woody, green tops and save them for soups and stews. (The green part remaining attached to the leek should be 4 to 6 inches long.)

Starting half an inch from the root plate, use a sharp knife to carefully split the leek lengthwise, leaving the root plate intact to hold the two parts together. Split all the way to the top of the leek, cutting through the remaining green portion. Carefully split each half again to get 4 long sections held together by the root plate.

Under running water, shake the leek gently like a cheerleader's pom-pom.

Lightly rub a large, cast-iron skillet with 1 tablespoon of the olive oil, and place the leeks in the skillet. Drizzle very lightly with the rest of the oil and sprinkle with sea salt.

Roast in the oven until leeks are frizzled, crisp, and lightly golden.

Serve with steaks.

Shallot S'mores

My decidedly grown-up version of a campfire favorite, this delectable hors d'oeuvre is a wonderful combination that will delight everyone from the fanciest culinary connoisseur to the most laid-back barbecue hostess. The quantity of ingredients needed to make these tasty treats depends entirely on your garden yield and the number of hungry guests you're feeding.

1 POUND FRESH SHALLOTS

2 TABLESPOONS EXTRA-VIRGIN OLIVE OIL

⅓ CUP FLAT-LEAF PARSLEY, MINCED

RYE CRACKERS

SOFT, MILD GOAT CHEESE

Wash shallots well and remove the skins; separate shallot lobes if necessary. Slice them into thin circles and separate into rings.

In a cast-iron skillet set over medium heat, warm the olive oil until lightly rippling. Add the shallot rings and sauté slowly, adding the parsley after 5 minutes. Continue cooking until shallots are limp and golden brown. Remove pan from heat, but keep warm.

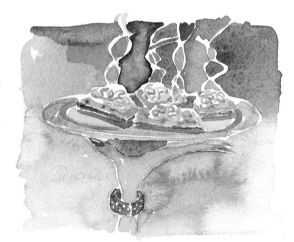

Spread rye crackers with a dollop of goat cheese. Top each cracker with a small spoonful of shallots and serve immediately.

Golden Carrot Soup

Bright orange in hue, this luscious soup is as stunning to look at as it is to eat; if you've got carrots in abundance, make a big batch and freeze a portion of it.

10 MEDIUM-SIZED FRESH CARROTS

2 TABLESPOONS UNSALTED BUTTER

1 LARGE SWEET ONION, MINCED

3 GARLIC CLOVES, PEELED AND MINCED

1 LARGE YUKON GOLD POTATO, UNPEELED AND CUT INTO CHUNKS

1½ TO 2 QUARTS CHICKEN BROTH OR STOCK

FRESH CARROT JUICE (SUCH AS ODWALLA BRAND)

SOUR CREAM AND PAPRIKA FOR SERVING

Remove the greens from the carrot tops and set aside for your compost bin. Scrub the carrots well, but do not peel them. Cut them into 2-inch chunks.

In a large soup pot set over medium-low heat, melt the butter, taking care to not let it brown. When the foam begins to subside, add the onions and the garlic, and sweat them until they're soft. Add the potato and the carrots to the pot, and barely cover with chicken broth.

Bring to a slow simmer, cover, and cook until all the vegetables are soft.

Remove three-quarters of the soup from the pot, and puree in a blender until smooth, adding carrot juice to achieve the right consistency. Return the puree to the soup pot and stir well.

Serve the soup hot or cold, topped with a dollop of sour cream and a dusting of good-quality paprika.

Beet-O-Rama

Redolent of earthy sweetness, beets are best served au naturel: *in other words, with as little done to them as possible! This recipe yields as many beets as your garden has given you to cook; make them in a big batch if necessary, since they're delicious sliced and served cold in a salad.*

FOR BEETS

FRESH GARDEN BEETS WITH THEIR GREENS

1 TABLESPOON EXTRA-VIRGIN OLIVE OIL

SEA SALT TO TASTE

FOR GREENS

2 TABLESPOONS EXTRA-VIRGIN OLIVE OIL

$^2/_3$ CUP MINCED ONION

2 GARLIC CLOVES, PEELED AND MINCED

3 PIECES BACON, CUT INTO 1-INCH PIECES

1 SMALL YUKON GOLD POTATO, UNPEELED AND CUBED

3 CUPS CHICKEN BROTH OR STOCK

FETA CHEESE FOR SPRINKLING

CIDER VINEGAR TO TASTE

FRESHLY GROUND BLACK PEPPER TO TASTE

Scrub the beets well, but do not peel them.

Remove the beet greens and set aside. Cut beets in half lengthwise.

Preheat oven to 350°F.

Brush a cast-iron skillet with $^1/_2$ tablespoon of the olive oil. Place the beets in the skillet, drizzle with the remaining $^1/_2$ tablespoon olive oil, and dust lightly with salt. Roast in the oven for 30–35 minutes, until they are soft enough to be pierced with a knife.

While the beets are roasting, wash the beet greens.

In a large cast-iron skillet set over medium heat, warm the olive oil until rippling but not smoking. Add the onion, garlic, and bacon, and toss to blend well.

Add the potato and just enough chicken broth to cover the mixture. Set a cover on the pan slightly askew, and cook at a low simmer until the potatoes are soft.

Add the beet greens to the pan, along with more chicken broth to just cover the greens. Firmly cover the pan and cook at a low simmer until the greens are tender.

When the beets are done, sprinkle them with feta cheese. When the greens have finished cooking, dress them with cider vinegar and freshly ground black pepper to taste. Serve the greens on a platter with the beets and feta spooned on top.

THIRTY-FIVE

ADD PERENNIAL EDIBLES

WHAT'S THE PAYOFF?

This small project explains how to grow four perennial edibles that will provide a yearly jump-start on harvesting food from your garden. Unlike lettuce, tomatoes, carrots, and other vegetables whose growing spots can change from year to year, each perennial edible is planted in one permanent spot and left there. French sorrel, rhubarb, and horseradish can be located within your salad garden or potager. A large stand of fiddlehead ferns may be grown anywhere on your property in any shady spot you like. These four perennial edibles will provide salads, soups, side dishes, condiments, and desserts for years, requiring very little work and almost no upkeep. (Sorrel, rhubarb, and horseradish have permanent locations in the potager planting plan on page 232. Asparagus is also a very popular perennial edible. Complete instructions for installing a dedicated asparagus bed, also included in the potager, follow in "Aspire to Asparagus," page 253.)

French sorrel is an uncommon, tangy, leafy vegetable. It can be picked as soon as it sprouts and the raw tender leaves added to the first of your spring salads. As the leaves grow larger, cut them back to the ground and use them as you would spinach to make a vitamin-packed springtime soup. (My favorite easy recipe is on page 252.)

Rhubarb is a delicious old-fashioned vegetable used for making old-fashioned pies. It is quicker to make a rhubarb pie than an apple pie, because you simply harvest the stems, cut off the green leafy part, and you're ready to go with no coring or peeling. And, of course, rhubarb is a great collaborator, combining with strawberries, blueberries, peaches, and other fruits to shared glory in your pie-making productions.

Fresh horseradish sauce was a favorite condiment on my grandmother's dining table. The long roots are dug up and grated raw into sour cream for the most fabulous accompaniment to the Easter lamb that you will ever taste. You can also smash grated fresh horseradish into cream cheese for serving on water biscuits as hors d'oeuvres. Although my grandmother would not have approved, grating fresh horseradish into Bloody Marys creates an unforgettable wake-up experience.

Fiddlehead ferns are very expensive and usually found only in gourmet groceries. Imagine my surprise when I discovered that the tall ostrich ferns planted on my shady dry bank were the source of this delicious treat. Since these ferns spread happily by underground stolons and quickly regenerate to replace picked fiddleheads, you can harvest an established patch often for plate-fuls of this decadent-seeming spring treat. Steam, sauté, or roast fiddleheads as you would asparagus.

PURCHASE PRIOR TO INSTALLATION
- French sorrel: 2 plants potted and ready to transplant
- Rhubarb: 2 plants potted and ready to transplant
- Horseradish: 2 plants potted and ready to transplant
- Ostrich fern (*Matteuccia struthiopteris*): at least 10 mature plants, potted and ready to transplant
- Sand: 1 very small bag

TOOLS
- Shovel
- Muck bucket
- Trowel

INSTALLATION
1. To plant sorrel: Choose a location in your garden where French sorrel can be grown permanently. If you have a small salad garden, choose 1 bed and place the 2 plants at opposite corners as decorative plumes of green. Or you may plant 1 sorrel plant dead center in 1 bed and 1 dead center in a matching bed. Or you may plant as per the potager plan on page 232.
2. Water the potted sorrel deeply and let sit for a few minutes while you dig the planting holes with a shovel. You do not need to amend the soil, as the garden soil is already amended.

3. Roll the pot on the ground firmly to remove the crown from the container. Do not pull the sorrel out by its leaves.

4. Place the crown of the sorrel plant at exactly the same level in the ground as in the pot. Replace soil, tamp down firmly, and water.

5. You may begin picking a few leaves as soon as you like. Cut leaves at ground level with sharp scissors.

6. To plant rhubarb: Allow room for these plants to spread out. A mature rhubarb plant will be about 2½ feet across. In a small salad garden, you can use rhubarb plants as focal points at the ends of your interior paths. Simply push back mulch, cut an X in the weed barrier cloth, and slip in the plant. Rhubarb's large leaves will shade out weeds that otherwise would sprout up underneath. Or plant as per the potager plan on page 232.

7. To transplant, water rhubarb deeply while still in its pot. Let this sit while you dig the holes for the plants.

8. Roll the pot on the ground to loosen the rhubarb from its container. Do not pull it out by its leaves.

9. Bury at exactly the same depth as the rhubarb was in its pot. You do not need to amend the soil.

10. Refill the hole and water in. Tamp down firmly.

11. Avoid picking rhubarb during its first growing season. The exception to this is if you have managed to purchase very large plants. In this case, try not to pick too many stems.

12. To harvest rhubarb, cut stems at ground level. Cut off the green part and compost. Cook stems only. Never eat green leaves, as they are poisonous. Although some cooks do, I do not peel my rhubarb. Chunked raw rhubarb freezes well.

13. To grow horseradish: The edible part is a long thin root that is dug up, so you should locate this plant where digging will not disturb other vegetables. Squeeze into the edge of a salad bed or follow the potager plan on page 232.

14. Water potted horseradish deeply and let sit for several minutes.

15. Dig a deep hole and remove the soil to a muck bucket.

16. Pour 2 handfuls of sand into the planting hole and mix with 1 handful of soil from the muck bucket. Horseradish is easier to dig up later if the soil is quite sandy.

17. Roll the pot firmly on the ground to loosen the plant. Be careful not to damage the long root.

18. Hold the root in the hole and backfill with sand and soil. Keep plant buried at the same level as it was in the container.

19. Water in and tamp down carefully.

20. Next spring when leaves have sprouted, use your weeding knife to dig up a piece of root. Store whole. Grate and use uncooked.

21. To grow fiddleheads: These ferns are beautiful edibles valuable for covering dry shady banks where few other ornamentals thrive. Choose a location where the ferns can naturalize and spread, as this will increase your yearly harvest.

22. Water ferns deeply in their pots and let sit. You will not need to dig deep holes, as these shallow-rooted ferns sit high out of the ground.

23. Roll the pot on the ground to loosen the fern. Once you see the size of the root and how it runs sideways, use a trowel to excavate the planting hole. Do not bury the knob where the fronds are attached. This sits out of the soil.

24. Allow about 1 foot between ferns when planting as they will soon fill in. Firm soil around plants with hands. Water well.

25. Let ferns spread for two seasons before harvesting.

26. To harvest: In the third spring, when a tightly coiled fiddlehead is 3 inches tall, snap off with your fingers. Store fiddle-heads in damp paper towels inside a plastic bag. Eat as soon as possible.

Easy French Sorrel Soup

*This bright green, refreshingly tangy soup is packed with vitamins . . . and flavor! It's a snap
to put together when the garden is exploding with this lovely vegetable.*

1½ TABLESPOONS UNSALTED BUTTER

3 GARLIC CLOVES, PEELED AND SMASHED WITH THE FLAT OF A KNIFE

1 SMALL ONION, PEELED AND COARSELY CHOPPED

2 MEDIUM YUKON GOLD POTATOES, CUBED BUT UNPEELED

CHICKEN BROTH TO COVER

1 PACKED CUP SHREDDED FRESH SORREL LEAVES

5 SPRIGS OF FLAT-LEAF PARSLEY

SOUR CREAM AND PAPRIKA FOR SERVING

In a medium soup pot, heat the butter until it just begins to foam. Add
the garlic cloves and the onion and cook until soft, about 6 to 8 minutes.

Add the cubed potatoes and barely cover with chicken broth. Set a
cover on the pan slightly askew, and simmer slowly, taking care to not let
the liquid evaporate below potato level.

When potatoes are soft, add the sorrel leaves and stir until wilted.

To puree, pour batches of the contents of the pot into a blender, add
more chicken broth if necessary,
and pulse until you've achieved
your desired consistency. Repeat
until all of the soup has been
pureed, adding the parsley at the
last pulsing to brighten the color.

Reheat and serve with a dollop
of sour cream sprinkled with
good-quality paprika.

THIRTY-SIX

WHAT'S THE PAYOFF?

This large project shows you how to establish an asparagus bed that will produce a decade's worth of delectable spears. Just-picked, crispy green asparagus is a tip-top gourmet treat, and the good news is that even a beginner gardener can aspire to have great asparagus.

The reason why some gardeners forgo asparagus is impatience: After planting, you must wait two more years before you get your first mouth-watering harvest. However, the intervening seasons require almost no work and, when your harvestable spears pop up the following spring, you will rejoice in your garden fortitude. Great asparagus is a grown-up garden accomplishment.

This project is the simple implementation of a three-year plan. While this sounds like a serious undertaking, in fact, there is little else that you can grow in your garden that is as amusing as asparagus. Year one, the baby plant looks really funny; year two, the teenager plant is endearingly gawky; and year three and afterward, you will laugh yourself silly over

ASPARAGUS AND SWEET PEAS

After your asparagus bed is mature, the hedge of fluffy foliage it will produce each summer makes a perfect natural trellis for growing fragrant, colorful sweet peas for unforgettable nosegays.

When the asparagus harvest season is over, plant sweet pea seeds along the long, east side of your bed. (I buy two packets of tall, old-fashioned scented types and plant as per packet instructions.) Just about the time that the vines need ways to climb, the foliage provides the means.

Planting on the east side of the asparagus keeps the sweet pea roots shaded from the hot afternoon sun, prompting them to flower longer into the summer. Keep picking to promote new buds.

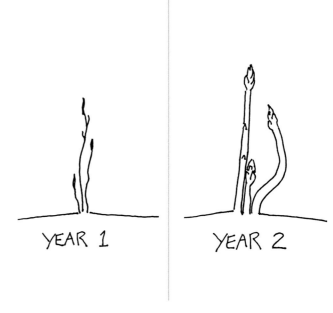

YEAR 1   YEAR 2

how much gourmet asparagus you will harvest. Our 14 x 3-foot bed of Jersey King asparagus annually produces about 25 pounds of the crispest, best-tasting asparagus imaginable—and will continue to do so for at least the next ten years. That is enough asparagus for four big eaters, plus several dinner parties, plus many giveaways. Now, that's good, clean fun!

This asparagus bed is cleared by using the Savvy Way for making a new bed described on page 16. The 14 x 3-foot bed is included in the potager plan on page 232, or you may plan this bed as a stand-alone perennial edible. Lay out the long side of the bed on a north-south orientation and make sure that the mature asparagus foliage, which billows six feet tall, will not shade out other plants.

If you have prepped the new asparagus bed over the winter as recommended in the Savvy Way, you will be right on target for a spring-

YEAR 3

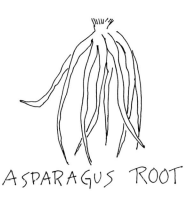

ASPARAGUS ROOT

TIPS FOR AN
EARLIEST
HARVEST

I don't like white asparagus at all, but I do use a variation of that technique to harvest a few very early spears. Use a plastic muck bucket that has (invariably) a broken bottom with holes in it. (The idea is to let light through the holes in the muck bucket bottom but to let the tall sides provide proctection.) Upturn the bucket over the sunniest part of your asparagus bed to make a cozy but light atmos-phere that encourages some early sprouting. (White asparagus is completely buried and sprouts in dark-ness to produce insipid sprouts devoid of health-giving greenness.)

time asparagus planting. Luckily, when the time was right to plant my asparagus crowns, in early May in my Zone 5, Mother's Day loomed and I asked for help digging out the bed as my present. Since a big trench eight inches deep and two feet wide must be excavated, I heartily recommend that you figure out something like this for your-self, too.

For planting, I recommend that you purchase year-old male asparagus crowns. Male asparagus plants do not produce berries that take nutrients away from the crown. The crown is a very odd structure with a rhizome and roots. It looks like a rubbery octopus. In a party game, no one would guess that this thing is where asparagus comes from.

But it does, and when the immature spears appear the second year, you will laugh again. Your second-spring asparagus will sprout very spindly, crooked foliage that doesn't look at all edible. You may even rue "who's the fool now," but remember that those who are patient reap the best rewards.

Finally, in its third year, you will go to your garden one morning and there will be beautiful asparagus popping up from bare soil like pencils poking up through a shoebox. It actually looks like a practical joke where your husband may have purchased a bunch of asparagus spears from the store and stuck them in the garden to fool you. But snap off your first spear and bite right into it and you'll realize why waiting is sometimes really worthwhile: This is no store-bought prank. This is simply the best asparagus you've ever tasted. Yes, this vegetable nirvana required some patience, but now you have years of rewards to reap.

PURCHASE PRIOR TO INSTALLATION
- 35–40-year-old male bare root asparagus crowns (My Jersey Kings came from Jersey Asparagus Farms, 609-358-2548. Local nurseries and farm-supply venues also sell bare root crowns.)
- 2 large plastic muck buckets
- Compost: enough to fill 14 x 3-foot trench 2 inches deep (order a delivery if you don't have enough of your own)
- Sturdy plastic tarp, as long as the bed (here, 14 feet)

TOOLS
- Shovel
- Trowel

INSTALLATION
1. Plot an asparagus bed 14 x 3 feet with a north-south orientation. Clear turf and weeds as per the Savvy Way on page 16.
2. To prepare planting trench: Place tarp along the length of the bed and begin digging, placing soil aside on top of tarp. The entire trench must be excavated 8 inches deep and 2 feet wide. Ideally,

2 people should begin working at either end of the bed and move toward meeting in the center. This is the most arduous part of the project and can be done in stages over several days.

3. Cover soil on tarp by folding tarp over onto the piles. This protects the soil from washing away during summer rains.

4. To plant: On planting day, fill muck buckets with the bare-root crowns. Add water to cover and allow crowns to soak for several hours.

5. Place 2 inches of compost in the trench. The trench will now be 6 inches deep.

6. Remove a crown from the water and gently spread the roots apart. Place in the trench. Do not cover yet.

7. Repeat and place a second crown 12 inches down the trench. Repeat, positioning crowns 12 inches apart to end of first row.

8. Do not cover yet.

9. The second row of crowns is staggered from the first. The first crown of the second row is placed in between the first 2 crowns initially planted (in an imaginary triangle), with all crowns 2 inches apart. Repeat until all crowns in second row are positioned. Jostle extras in, trying to maintain recommended distances.

10. When all the crowns are in the trench, gently water in and cover with 2 inches of the soil reserved on the tarp. That's it for now.

11. First year: Asparagus bed should receive 1 inch of water per week. Use an inexpensive rain gauge and supplement with sprinklers as needed. After the first year, asparagus develops very deep roots and does not require extra watering.

12. First year: Around July, the baby asparagus will have sprouted weak, colt-ish stems and foliage. With the reserved soil under the tarp, carefully pat 2 inches of soil in and around the plants, taking care that the fluffy part is above the soil line.

13. First year: In August or September, add the final 2 inches of soil from the tarp to completely fill the bed. (Remove and store tarp for later uses.)

14. First autumn: Leave foliage intact for winter.
15. Second spring: Cut down and compost all old foliage in early spring. Sprinkle bed with compost. Refrain from harvesting.

HOW MUCH TO HARVEST?

The standard recommendations for harvesting asparagus:
- *Third year: Pick all spears for two weeks*
- *Fourth year: Pick all spears for four weeks*
- *Fifth year: Pick all spears for six weeks*
- *Sixth and onward: As above*

16. Second summer: Watch for dreaded, gross asparagus beetle larvae. These tiny black worms can be sprayed with insecticidal soap early on a windless morning. Be diligent.
17. Second autumn: Leave foliage intact over winter.
18. Third spring: Remove old foliage. Sprinkle bed with compost.
19. Third spring: Harvest! Snap off 7- to 10-inch-tall spears crisply with your fingers. Leave stubs alone. *(See "How Much to Harvest?")*
20. Third spring: Store extra spears in crisper section of fridge. Rinse, wrap in a clean dishtowel, and place in a plastic bag.
21. Subsequent years: You should know the drill by now.

Truffled Asparagus with Shirred Eggs, Pecorino-Toscano, and Pepper

There are certain earthy ingredients that wind up being absolutely heavenly when put together: Combine fresh asparagus with white truffle oil (or, if the coffers are fuller than usual, fresh white truffles from Alba), a fresh egg or two, and a Pecorino-Toscano, and the result is simple and spectacular. Make this for a special breakfast or have it for dinner with a chilled bottle of crisp white wine, like a nice Sancerre.

10–12 FRESH ASPARAGUS STALKS (HERE, THICKER IS BETTER), WOODY
    ENDS SNAPPED OFF

$^1\!/_2$ TABLESPOON EXTRA-VIRGIN OLIVE OIL

$^1\!/_4$ TEASPOON SEA SALT

$^1\!/_4$ TEASPOON WHITE TRUFFLE OIL

1–3 FRESH EGGS

FRESHLY CRACKED BLACK PEPPER

PECORINO-TOSCANO, FOR SHAVING

Preheat the oven to 400°F.

Toss the asparagus in a medium cast-iron pan with olive oil and sea salt.

Place in the oven for 5 minutes, then lower the heat to 375°F and continue to cook for another 5 to 8 minutes (depending on the thickness), until almost tender.

Remove the pan from the oven and drizzle the stalks with truffle oil. Gently crack 1 to 3 eggs directly over the asparagus, taking care not to break the yolks. Return the pan to the oven and cook until the yolks are just set.

Serve hot, with cracked black pepper to taste and a few shavings of fresh Pecorino-Toscano.

V.

KEEP ON GOING AND NEVER STOP GROWING: CELEBRATE THE SEASONS

B esides identifying myself as a gardener, I also am quick to call myself a gypsy. I adore traveling, especially for work, because, well, get a group of gardening people together and there will never be a dull moment. In some parts of the country, nongardeners might initially inquire, "Who are you people?" but gardeners everywhere always begin a conversation with "What is your zone?" Gardeners love to hear what is going on with their buddies in other climatic zones and, sometimes, like to boast a bit about the beauty of autumn foliage, the ease of outdoor tropical orchids, or the blessings of reliable snow coverage. America is a huge country and, lucky us, we have many ways to talk to one another about our various seasons and what appeals to us about each one.

I have been fortunate to have had gardens in Zones 5, 6, 7, and whatever semi-tropical zone southwestern England includes. (Can you imagine in-ground palm trees in latitudes north of New York City? Welcome to winter in Exeter, England!) Besides our garden in Garrison, New York, part of my family has also begun a garden in Pasadena, California. In Garrison my rosemary is an annual; in Pasadena the hedge is rosemary. In Garrison we have snow for Christmas; in Pasadena we have roses.

This section of the book celebrates the seasons in as many permutations as possible. Although spring begins at different times in different places, it is always a welcome season. Your local climate dictates whether the treasures of summer are long-lasting or romantically fleeting, and my list of tough, little fall-planted bulbs is widely adaptable throughout a huge part of the country. Winter is a bit more specific, but even if you never have icy weather, in this section you will also learn about the joys of snow and, perhaps, gain insight into why it has its own appeal. And, finally, for anyone who loves gardening to a degree that it's sometimes tough to go inside, the final section here is for all who find a tabletop just too bare without a plant (or twenty).

This section describes how to plan for and happily anticipate seasonality.

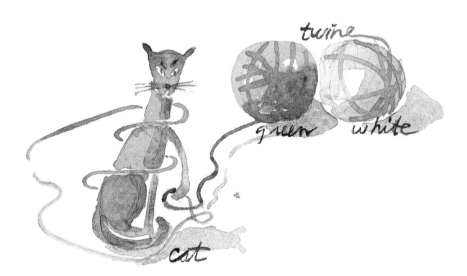

THIRTY-SEVEN

WHAT'S THE PAYOFF?

This small project satisfies the urge to make your garden attractive in early spring. Tulips, daffodils, snowdrops, and all the other spring-blooming bulbs are the perennial treasures of the season, but these little jewels had to have been buried during the previous autumn. *(See "Fall into Bulbs," page 273.)* But don't despair if you haven't been able to get around to that autumn activity yet, because here you'll learn how to quickly perk up your outdoor space at the same moment spring rolls out her green carpet.

You'll learn here how to add a few very hardy spring bloomers to your garden as soon as the ground thaws. Plants with very early displays are listed below, and planning and planting instructions for a spring border spot are in the installation directions.

Choose a location near the house to spotlight the season, as the likelihood of you traveling far afield during this chilly time is remote. There's no point in creating a sweet waterside springtime spot with primroses, bleeding hearts, and violets if it's too wet or chilly to go out to the pond to see it.

If you are just thinking about a garden and don't have any beds yet, you can still enjoy this project. Simply purchase any of the plants here and keep them in their plastic nursery pots. Slip the nursery pots inside more decorative clay containers and arrange a sweet spring welcome right next to the front door. A pussy willow shrub, hardy ferns, colorful primulas, and other spring bloomers will all carry on with their spring-time shows as long as you keep them watered just as you would any other containerized plants. You may add these plants to your beds and borders later on as your garden grows, or you can simply treat them as one-off pleasures.

The trick to enjoying this tiny project is to remember that this is more about the promise of a garden to come rather than anything larger or too elaborate. For this spring, keep it small and simple and smile.

PERENNIALS WITH EARLY SHOW

- ⁕ bleeding hearts (Dicentra spectabilis)
- ⁕ lungwort (Pulmonaria spp.)
- ⁕ Virginia bluebells (Mertensia virginiana)
- ⁕ violets
- ⁕ ferns
- ⁕ Euphorbia spp.

PURCHASE PRIOR TO INSTALLATION

- Primroses: Buy as many as you like, and treat as annuals. If planted in the garden, they may perennialize and return next spring.
- Pansies: The smaller pansies like Johnny-jump-up may perennialize. Larger pansies probably will not return next year.
- Perennials: Buy early-blooming perennials in odd numbers (3, 5, etc.) as space allows.
- Early-blooming shrub: 1
- Small evergreen: 1
- OPTIONAL: Containers. If display will be kept in nursery pots, purchase attractive containers large enough to slip plastic pots inside.
- OPTIONAL: Garden table or picnic bench, to show off pots near front door.

TOOLS

- Trowel

INSTALLATION

1. To make a small spring spot in an existing border: Choose a location near the front door or one that is easily visible. Clear away winter debris.

2. Use a trowel to dig all planting holes. A small digging tool allows a margin of error in case you accidentally dig up a dormant border plant. If this happens, apologize and simply press the preexisting plant firmly back into place. Move over a bit and gently dig another hole for your new addition.

3. Transplant the spring-blooming shrub first. Position at rear of border. *(See "Slip in Some Shrubs," page 138.)*

4. Transplant evergreen pieris, juniper, or boxwood next. Position either left or right in front of first shrub. Plant closely so that early blooms of the first shrub will eventually have a background of evergreen branches.

5. Transplant perennials in triangle shapes based on the positions of the transplanted flowering shrub and evergreen. For example: Plant 3 bleeding hearts in a triangle next to a triangle of Virginia bluebells. Keep these as close to the shrubs as possible for the best visual effect.

6. Scatter primroses and pansies as desired among other transplants. In springtime, a riot of color is very cheerful.

7. OPTIONAL: Take snapshot of your spring scene and keep this in your garden records. It will serve as an autumn reminder if you wish to add fall-planted tulips and daffodils to your springtime spot.

8. If springing forward in containers, slip all plastic nursery pots inside decorative containers. Make

EARLY-BLOOMING SHRUBS

- *forsythia*
- *corylopsis*
- *abeliophyllum*
- *pussy willow*
- *fothergilla*
- *witch hazel*
- *bridal wreath spirea*
- *red-twig dogwood*

SMALL EVERGREEN SHRUBS

- *dwarf pieris*
- *dwarf boxwood*
- *prostrate juniper*

sure that the decorative pot can drain so that the plastic pot does not sit in water.

9. Arrange containerized plants on the front porch, marching up steps, beside a garden bench located near the house, or relocate a picnic bench close to the front door to use as a stage.

10. After flowering is complete, consider transplanting your containerized spring bloomers into the ground. Hopefully, this will constitute the thin end of the wedge that gets your garden going.

WHAT'S THE PAYOFF?

This small project shows you how to enhance your summer garden with spring-planted bulbs. When most people think about bulbs, they consider only the autumn-planted types—tulips, daffodils, crocus, and so on—that bloom in springtime. But there are many bulbs that can be planted early in the growing season to cause a blooming ruckus of summer color and fragrance only a few months later. This project explains how to grow the three easiest types of summer-blooming bulbs and, at the end, offers a list of additional treats that can also serve as summer's buried treasures.

Celebrate a seasonal splash of bulbs with specially selected lilies, sweetly perfumed acidantheras, and bursts of outrageous color from dahlias. All of these bulbs are inexpensive, readily available, simple to grow, and shine as showstoppers in the summer garden. Additionally, all the bulbs here may be grown in containers.

LILIES FOR SPRING PLANTING

There are hundreds of different lilies, but for this project, you should choose the types listed below that grow roots from buried stems. These stem-rooting lilies will bloom the same year that they are planted.

Choose from each group listed to get the longest succession of flowers. Lilies are perennials and all of these are hardy in cold areas. (All bulbs listed here are from Brent and Becky's Bulbs; see page 275.)

Early blooming: 'Vivaldi', 'Citronella', 'Jacqueline'

Midseason blooming: 'Clubhouse', 'African Queen', 'Pink Perfection'

Late blooming: 'Black Beauty', 'Casa Blanca', 'La Reve'

Species types: L. formosanum, L. henryi, L. martagon

PURCHASE PRIOR TO INSTALLATION

- Lily bulbs: at least 6 of each, as many types as desired *(see sidebar at left)*
- Acidanthera corms: at least 24 *(see sidebar, opposite)*
- Dahlia tubers: at least 3 of each, as many types as desired
- OPTIONAL: Pots, potting soil, and sand if desired for container planting

TOOLS

- Trowel
- Plant markers and indelible-ink pen

INSTALLATION

1. Purchase all bulbs and store in a dark, cool place (not the fridge) until planting times outlined below.
2. For lilies in ground: In March, plant bulbs in individual holes 10 inches deep. (Depth is crucial, as roots will form along the stem as it pushes upward from the bulb.) Mark location with plant marker to avoid disturbing it later.
3. Lilies planted in the ground will overwinter with no extra protection.
4. Lilies in containers: Containers must be deep enough to allow the bulb to be buried 10 inches. Potting mixture should have plenty of sand for good drainage.
5. Lilies planted in pots can be transplanted into the ground in autumn after flowering is complete.
6. If lilies are kept from year to year in pots, store pots on their sides under porch or in garage to prevent breakage from freezing.

7. To plant acidantheras: These corms are planted after the last frost of spring. (This is the same time tomato plants go outside, around June 1 in my Zone 5.)

8. Acidantheras in the ground: The little corms are planted just below the surface of the soil. Place closely together in shallow holes for blooming impact. Replace soil and pat surface of soil firmly with your hand to secure the corm in ground. Mark position with a plant marker. Plant where night perfumes can be enjoyed.

9. Acidantheras in pots: Plant shallowly in well-draining potting mixture with added sand.

10. Acidantheras are hardy in Zones 8 and above. If this isn't you, purchase new corms every year.

11. To plant dahlias: These tubers are planted after the last frost, at the same time as tomatoes (and acidantheras) are planted outside. This is around June 1 in my Zone 5 garden.

12. Dahlias in the ground: Plant tubers about 4 inches deep, with eyes pointing up. (The eyes are bumps that will produce stems.) Allow about 12 inches between tubers, as dahlias are bushy plants.

13. Dahlias in pots: Plant in quick-draining potting medium with sand added for extra drainage. Plant as described in step 12.

14. When dahlia plant has 3 sets of leaves, pinch shoots back to encourage branching. Repeat pinching process 2 weeks later.

15. OPTIONAL: To give dahlias a head start in cold regions, start indoors 1 month before last frost. (May 1 is the start date in my Zone 5.) Transplant head-start dahlia plants into the garden in June.

WHAT IS AN ACIDANTHERA?

Acidantheras, grown in gardens for more than a century, are statuesque, white flowers with dark purple markings. They are sweetly perfumed after sunset.

The little bulbs (more correctly called corms) produce flowers about three feet tall. Sometimes called peacock orchid, magpie gladiolus, Gladiolus callianthus, and probably a few other names, these bulbs may be unfamiliar to some, but once you try them, their graceful forms and sweet perfumes will become a favorite part of your summer.

Acidanthera corms are sold in packets in ordinary garden centers or they can be mail-ordered from Brent and Becky's Bulbs (see page 275). They are hardy only in Zones 8–11, but are so inexpensive (50 for $15) they can be purchased fresh every spring.

DALLIANCE WITH DAHLIAS

Misguided gardeners steer clear of dahlias because they fear the need to dig and store the tubers in winter. Guess what? No one cares if you let them freeze to death. Then you'll have room to try different ones each year.

If you fall in love with a particular dahlia, overwintering the tubers is a simple, quick task and is explained in step 17.

OTHER BURIED TREASURES

- *begonias*
- *caladiums*
- *elephant ears*
- *cannas*
- *crocosmias*
- *alstroemerias*
- *summer hyacinths*
- *gladioli*
- *gingers*
- *four o'clocks*
- *tuberoses*

16. Dahlias are hardy in Zones 8 or higher. For colder areas, either purchase fresh tubers each year or see the next step.

17. OPTIONAL: To keep (overwinter) dahlia tubers: After the first frost, gently dig up tubers with a hand fork. Do not wash off the soil. Do not cut off foliage. Place dug plants in a single layer on newspapers in a dry, warm place indoors. After a week, foliage will wither and excess soil can be brushed away. Cut off leaves, leaving a few inches of the stems attached to the tuber. Store tubers in paper bags in basement or other dark area with temperatures around 45 degrees.

THIRTY-NINE

Fall Into Bulbs

WHAT'S THE PAYOFF?

This large project explains how to plant five hundred inexpensive, unusual, small bulbs that will burst into bloom next spring from February until May. First to bloom, even if snow is still falling where you live, will be a white, purple, and yellow medley of snowdrops, crocus, and baby yellow iris near the front door. For beds and borders there are small blue grape hyacinths and more tiny irises with thin, delicate leaves that don't turn into messy mayhem later. For the lawn, a scattering of scilla sapphires will sparkle under still-bare tree branches. This will be followed by purple and white checked antiquities that are happy in any place you plant them. Months later, spring's blooms will crescendo in a splash of wild tulips and daffodils that will overlap with the emergence of the rest of your garden.

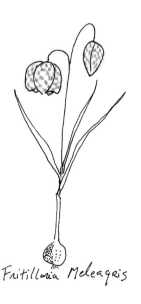

Fritillaria Meleagris

KATHERINE'S RECOMMENDED 500-BULB ORDER

For early white, purple, and yellow bloom medley:

- ❧ *Snowdrop* (Galanthus *spp.*): *50, very early nodding white flowers*
- ❧ *Crocus: 50, very early, try 'Remembrance', 'Vanguard', or 'Paulus Potter' for great purple color*
- ❧ Iris danfordiae: *50, very early, tiny, fragrant, bright yellow*

For blues that behave in beds and borders:

- ❧ *Grape hyacinth* (Muscari armeniacum*): 50, beautiful blue, lightly fragrant*
- ❧ Iris reticulata: *50, like blue dragonflies, 'Edward', 'Harmony', or 'Gordon'*

For tiny sapphires in the lawn:

- ❧ Scilla siberica *'Spring Beauty': 100, small enough to be jabbed into lawn with knife, so early and small that lawn can be mowed later as needed*

Little antiquities for anywhere:

- ❧ *Checkered lily* (Fritillaria meleagris*): 100, small purple and white checked bells on bluish-green stems, will tolerate wet, cold, shade, poor soil, a crowd-stopper*

Splash of wild tulips and daffodils:

- ❧ Tulipa batalinii *'Bronze Charm': 20, petite, bronzy yellow, fragrant, small beautiful leaves with waved edges*
- ❧ Tulipa humilis *'Persian Pearl': 10, short, dark magenta and purple, compact dark foliage*
- ❧ *Pheasant's Eye daffodil* (Narcissus poeticus *var.* recurvus): *20, the last to bloom, but what a way to go! Bulbs are bigger and need deeper holes, but worth it, white petals, small yellow cup with red rim, very fragrant.*

Crocus

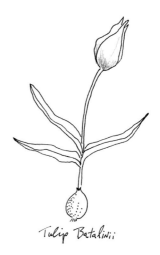

Tulip Batalinii

All the bulbs I recommend here have wide hardiness ranges and are very inexpensive to purchase. I grow them all successfully despite being in a high-critter area. Deer, moles, and voles don't seem to go for these tiny treats like they do for the bigger sweets. Additionally, all can be expected to perennial-ize and return to cheer up many future springtimes. Although some of these bulbs are not generally found in local nurseries, all are available by mail order.

As they are shipped in a completely dormant state, bulbs offer the perfect opportunity for mail-ordering. You can order bulbs anytime after you receive your catalogs and they will be sent to you at their optimal planting moment. (This last service takes away the worry of when to plant your autumn bulbs.) Personally, I buy almost all my bulbs from the three catalogs listed at right, my favorites.

The general rule of thumb regarding planting bulbs is that they should be buried at least three times as deep as the actual bulb is tall (the bulb itself, not the

PLANT BULBS AS DEEP AS 3 TIMES THEIR HEIGHT

Tulip Bulb

MY FAVORITE BULB MAIL-ORDER SOURCES

- *Brent and Becky's Bulbs: Family-owned since 1900, unbeatable selection, fully photographed catalog, wonderful people. www.brentand-beckysbulbs.com or 877-661-2852.*

- *John Scheepers: Company is 90 years old, with great catalog, well photographed. www.johnscheepers.com or 860-567-0838.*

- *Old House Gardens: Company began in 1993 to specialize in heirloom bulbs, great catalog, wonderful choices, fascinating information. www.oldhousegardens.com or 734-995-1486.*

flower that will eventually emerge). Since a big tulip bulb can be 3 inches tall or more, this means digging multiple holes at least 9 inches deep. That's a lot of digging. The little bulbs in this project are so small that their holes only need to be 2½ to 3 inches deep. If you scoop out holes 6 or 8 inches wide, you can plant 25 bulbs in one spot. This technique makes your autumn planting go much faster, and these babies look better when many are planted together.

PURCHASE PRIOR TO INSTALLATION

- 500 bulbs: as listed above, or substitute as desired

TOOLS

- Scissors
- Garden basket
- Weed knife
- Trowel, good quality, non-bending
- Shovel
- Plastic flower pots: gallon size, tape over hole
  or Small bucket
- Wooden plant markers and indelible-ink pen

INSTALLATION

1. Use scissors to cut open bulb bags. Leave bulbs in open bags. Place all bags and plant markers in a basket. Save each bag and its label as you plant. Use indelible ink to write bulb location on the bag label.
2. For earliest medley near porch: Use trowel to plant snowdrops, crocuses, and baby irises in clusters near the front porch.
3. Place excavated soil in plastic pot or small bucket as you dig. This makes replacing soil very easy.
4. Dig all holes at same time, position at least 10 bulbs of the same type of flower in each hole. Do not mix different types. Do not replace soil yet.

5. Make plant markers, one for each type, and place them in appropriate holes. It is not necessary to mark every hole, as it will be obvious which flowers are identical.

6. When all bulbs are nestled in holes, replace soil in all holes and pat down firmly.

7. Water well now and over the next few weeks if no rain falls.

8. For blues that behave in borders: Choose border position near front or midway back for ease of viewing. Make wide shallow holes. Shape holes like big teardrops with the narrow end near the front of the border. Avoid planting in rows.

9. Follow planting guides above in steps 3–7, planting grape hyacinths and small blue irises in separate clusters.

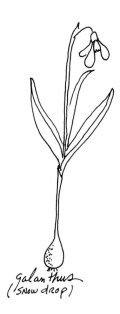

Galanthus
('Snow drop')

10. For scilla sapphires in the lawn: Select a lawn area near the house. To plant scillas, stab a weed knife into the ground and lever soil and grass open. There is no need to remove the soil or grass, just push it aside and hold. Push a scilla bulb into opening, remove the weed knife, and push soil and grass back in place. Step on top firmly. Repeat until all scillas are planted. No need to mark. Water well if no rain falls.

11. For little antiquities: To plant small frittilaries, use same planting technique as for scillas above. Frits can go in the lawn, under trees, in borders, in wet areas, near the porch, or in front of shrubs. Plant singly or in clusters. Water if needed.

12. Wild tulips: Plant in position of honor in border. Use trowel to excavate holes as described in steps 3–7, *except* plant 5 bulbs in each hole. Do not mix 'Bronze Charm' and 'Persian Pearl' in same hole, but place them near each other. Mark with wooden markers.

13. Pheasant's Eye daffodils: You will need a shovel to plant these bulbs.

Choose a spot where ripening foliage won't be unsightly, i.e., near the edge of pond, at the edge of the woods, or at the back of the border. Dig 2 big holes for 10 bulbs each. Water holes and let soak in. Position bulbs firmly, refill holes, and tamp soil firmly. Mark position with wooden markers.

14. Save all descriptive material from bags, labels, and catalogs. When you can, enter this information into your garden records *(see "Record Your Progress" on page 32.)*

15. OPTIONAL: Photograph your spring-flowering bulbs and keep snaps in your garden records. This will show you where to add more bulbs next fall.

FORTY

Welcome Winter

WHAT'S THE PAYOFF?

This small project teaches you how to create a winter beauty spot outside your favorite window. Snow and ice can actually be put to work in your garden, defining the lacy greenery of pines, sugar-glazing the fringed yellow blossoms of witch hazel, or making red viburnum berries look like blown glass beads. White snow and winter-blue skies create Wedgwood settings for the strong shadows cast by bare trees. Cragged dogwood bark or black rudbeckia seed heads catch the tiniest fluffs of snow and invite the same close inspection as summer's most fetching roses. Creating a welcome to winter shows that you, an enthusiastic, energetic gardener, enjoy the garden every month of the year—even if under snow from November until April.

Since most nurseries are closed during the winter months, this project provides especially good lessons in sophisticated plant selection. Winter garden areas must be planted during the growing season, so your challenge is to purchase plants with advance knowledge of their added

off-season value. Plants with multi-seasonal beauty are often called "four-season plants."

Four-season plants usually march through twelve months flaunting some or all of the following characteristics: appealing flowers, colorful autumn foliage, interesting bark, pretty berries or fruit, and intriguing shapes. Some annuals and perennials are considered four-season plants because the skeletons they leave behind add sculptural forms to snowy landscapes.

Unless you have a very small urban space, there is no point in winter-beautifying your entire garden. Instead, follow the suggestion here and pick a likely spot—for example, the view from the living room window—and make it pretty for daytime and evening enjoyment. The theme of this project might be summed up as "Winter happens: Make it wonderful!"

PURCHASE PRIOR TO INSTALLATION DATE

- Dwarf evergreen shrub: 1, spire shaped, about 5 feet tall (arborvitae and cypress are good choices)
- Small evergreen: one, preferably with a round shape (a dwarf rhododendron, azalea, boxwood, holly, or mugo pine would work)
- Low, flat evergreen: 1 (a prostrate blue spruce, thyme, or ivy will be fine)
- Four-season deciduous shrub: 2 or 3 (viburnum, witch hazel, wigelia, vitex, winterberry, and pyracantha are good choices)
- Border plants: 3 or more with winter skeletons (sea oat grass, rudbeckias, baptisias, verbascums, and asters persist until the end of winter)
- Small white outdoor lights: 1 string

TOOLS

- Shovel
- Trowel

INSTALLATION

1. To design a beauty spot: Assemble your purchased plants and begin arranging them (still in their pots) outside your chosen window. If you are working in an existing border, you may need to consider moving some established plantings to another location. There is no problem with this: Remember that all plants have "wheels." Do not worry about planting distances. Close plantings produce glorious results quickly.

2. Maneuver the potted plant material and think of your potential design in terms of overlapping triangles. For example, place the

FOUR-SEASON PLANT MATERIAL

- *arborvitae*
- *cypress*
- *rhododendron*
- *mountain laurel*
- *azalea*
- *boxwood*
- *holly*
- *mugo pine*
- *peegee hydrangea*
- *prostrate blue spruce*
- *Adam's needle*
- *yucca*
- *sedum 'Autumn Joy'*
- *ivy*
- *viburnum*
- *witch hazel*
- *wigelia*
- *staghorn sumac*
- *vitex*
- *winterberry*
- *pyracantha*
- *ornamental grass*
- *rudbeckia*
- *baptisia*
- *verbascum*
- *aster*
- *Queen Anne's lace*

INSPIRING
WINTER SCENERY

If you've never seen a great winter beauty spot, it might be difficult to imagine the appeal. Leafing through a few books dedicated to the subject is a great way to inspire your creativity. The first two books have beautiful photographs and many detailed plant lists.

The Unsung Season: Gardens and Gardeners in Winter by Sydney Eddison (Houghton Mifflin, 1995).

The Garden in Winter by Rosemary Verey (Little, Brown and Company, 1988).

I also recommend that Southern gardeners seek out the vintage classic Gardens in Winter by North Carolina writer Elizabeth Lawrence.

taller spire-shaped evergreen to the rear, off center, and snuggle in one of the deciduous shrubs. If pyracantha is the deciduous shrub you have chosen, imagine how the berries will look against the evergreens later on. To complete the first planting triangle, place the grass as the third point of the triangle.

3. Using the above suggested triangle as a foundation, move other potted plants into position. For example, set the low-growing evergreen at the foot of the grass and the rudbeckia (which will have tall, thin black stems throughout winter) to the right of that green island.

4. The rounded evergreen (for example, a boxwood ball) can anchor another overlapping triangle to the left with perennial asters and the low-mounded evergreen as the other points. You should now have 7 plants in their potential planting positions.

5. At this point, pause and go inside. Look out the chosen window at your potential winter-beauty spot. Are all the plants visible from indoors? If not, you may need to move everything out a bit farther. Can you see (in your mind's eye) if the rudbeckia stems will be close enough to the grass plumes? If not, move the rudbeckia closer to the grass. Does the design look natural or do you need to push a few pots askew to avoid a soldiers-in-formation look?

6. Go back outside and make adjustments, adding the rest of your purchased plant material until the design looks complete. Leftovers can be added to borders elsewhere.

7. After you have positioned all plant material, checked from inside, repositioned, and rechecked from inside, begin planting your purchases.

8. Dig holes and work from the house outward so that the taller items are not in your way as you work. Unpot and plant according to "Plant Perennial Pleasures," page 133, and "Slip in Some Shrubs," page 138.

9. Once all plants are in, check your results from outside looking toward the house. You might want to complete your design with a few balancing plants that will be unseen from inside, but that will make the work fit better when viewed from the garden.

10. Keep all plants watered and maintained throughout the growing season, as per the suggestions in "Water Wisely," page 57.

11. In autumn: Be careful when cleaning up your borders. Make sure to leave the grass plumes and plant skeletons intact, but tidy the adjoining area.

12. Winter: This is the season of long nights. A string of small white outdoor lights can be positioned like a diamond necklace through the branches of your winter beauty spot. Turning the lights on will become part of your evening ritual, a little moment to look out and to reflect upon the undaunted beauty of winter. Penny for penny, I bet those little lights will bring you more pleasure than a diamond necklace ever will.

OTHER SOURCES OF WINTER BEAUTY

We leave many of our garden ornaments outside in winter. Obelisks, the sundial, concrete objects, metal tuteurs, and topiary forms look far more expensive when they have gotten a bit weathered and dented. This benign neglect eventually produces patina. The short-term payoff is that you don't need to haul things in and out of storage and your garden will have interesting forms for snow to drape and ice to glaze.

FORTY-ONE

WHAT'S THE PAYOFF?

This small project shows how to create and maintain a stylish indoor garden. Although this book is dedicated to the larger outdoor landscape, a person with a well-chosen and well-designed indoor garden can putter among plants when outdoor conditions are not salubrious. Also, a manageable indoor garden makes a wonderful present to give to someone who lives in a high-rise or who finds it difficult to work outdoors. Here you'll learn to make a stylish tabletop garden of great-looking plants that brings a true sense of the living garden indoors.

It must be said that the word "houseplants" sometimes sets off Bad Taste Detectors. Too many people have painful memories of awful aunties in parlors packed with moldering African violets. Thankfully, today's indoor garden has moved miles beyond that particular terror. Today's gardeners care about design and content, and their indoor gardens reflect their artistic plant passions.

INDOOR PLANTS
THAT LIKE SHADE

- ferns
- begonias
- selected orchids
- coleus
- hibiscus
- flowering maple
- ivy
- primroses

INDOOR PLANTS
FOR A SUNNY,
DRY ATMOSPHERE

- cacti
- hens and chicks
- succulents
- agaves
- aeonium
- pelargoniums
- herbs
- scented geraniums

There are no huge secrets for successful indoor gardening. The first step toward greatness is simple: Pick plants that will love your interior conditions. If your sunlight is limited, go the fabulous ferns and beautiful begonia route. (I don't like grow lights as décor: They hint of the surgical theater.) If your indoor climate is hot and dry, look for unusual succulents, agaves, and flowering cacti. If you want orchids, these require more atmospheric moisture, but there are some that love sunlight and some that love shade. To buy a plant perfect for your house, simply check the nursery tags before purchasing and don't fudge on what conditions you really have to offer.

Indoor humidity and air quality are factors that are easy to adjust. Use a humidifier, place trays of water on radiators, and position beautiful bowls of water in your tabletop garden. You'll discover that the water you offer evaporates so quickly that containers may need to be refilled daily during the winter heating months.

Indoor atmospheres sometimes tend to stagnate, especially when it is impossible to open windows. An inexpensive table fan makes a tremendous difference in plant health by circulating stagnant air. Set the fan on the floor. Point it up toward the ceiling and away from plants. A fan blowing directly on plants will eventually dry out leaves and flowers too much. Once you add humidity and circulating air to your indoor garden, you will discover that both small adjustments enhance conditions for humans and plants alike.

The final key to indoor garden success has been documented endless times: Most indoor plants die from overwatering and overfertilizing. Once you learn to curb your overenthusiasm as per the instructions below, your garden is already off to a better start.

As you begin your indoor garden plant collection, you'll find that most plants first arrive at your house in plastic. So did your lampshades. You immediately threw away the lampshade plastic and you need to ditch the cheesy pots pronto. Your indoor garden is a display area and every plant deserves a beautiful pot.

This project urges you to arrange all your plants in one main area to create a fuller garden effect. Since most windowsills are very narrow, use a table or bench placed in front of the window to allow for depth of design and more plant presence. One plant here and one plant over there does not make a splashy outdoor scene, and the same is true indoors. Additionally, if you group plants together in one place, you can more easily take perfect care of them because watering, fertilizing, and primping all happen in one spot.

Just as in your outdoor garden, your indoor garden will benefit from designing with good color choices and interesting plant forms. Your local nursery, a specialized greenhouse, and even most ordinary Home-Mega-Stores now have extensive greenhouse collections. Assemble a collection of indoor plants that please you and that will be pleased by your conditions. For example, a cactus is not just a green spiky thing. Many have long-lasting colorful blooms. A tall cactus with a red cap would look terrific next to a leafy aeonium that has red in its foliage. Add a round blue agave and a few trailing gray succulents and you are starting to create an indoor garden for a hot sunny spot.

Once you have your favorite plants in great pots, arrange them so that the collection looks like a little garden. As in your outdoor garden, place taller things in the back, group plants in odd numbers, and think about what colors look good with what other colors. Topiary trees, vines on small tuteurs, trailing plants, spiky plants, fragrant plants, and big bloomers should be arranged and rearranged until each one benefits from its position and its context.

INDOOR PLANTS
THAT REQUIRE
SOME HUMIDITY

- *orchids*
- *ferns*
- *calla lily*
- *begonias*
- *coleus*
- *citrus*
- *potted bulbs*
- *jasmine*

My tabletop indoor garden also has a lamp on it, places for a few candles, big and small bowls of water, a tiny Buddha, some seashells, and various other sentimental tidbits. These ornamental objects are quirky and personal and, hopefully, move my home horticulture from the dreaded realm of houseplants and into the world of personalized gardening. As a final suggestion, once you make your indoor garden, move a comfortable chair next to your happy plants and indulge in Edenic catnaps. It's a great way to enjoy your garden efforts.

PURCHASE PRIOR TO INSTALLATION

- Inexpensive waterproof table or bench (metal, stone outdoor table, tiled table, picnic bench, etc.) to fit desired space
- Heavy-gauge plastic sheeting (to protect the floor under the table from water)
- Inexpensive absorbent rug to hide plastic sheeting (cotton rag rugs are great)
- Inexpensive metal serving trays, flea market serving platters, plates, bowls, saucers, etc. (for preventing drips under pots and filling with water for evaporation)
- Small watering can with a long pointed tip
- Small container of liquid plant fertilizer for foliage
- Small container of liquid plant fertilizer bloom booster
- Plastic hand sprayer with mist and jet action
- Plants: at least 5 (choose location first, then purchase plants accordingly)
- Containers: for plants purchased
- Potting mix: enough for transplanting into containers
- Sand: small bag
- Compost: small bag
- Galvanized washtub or other container to fit under table and hold all supplies

TOOLS

- Empty plastic 1-gallon milk jugs: 2
- Inexpensive spoon
- Knife
- Scissors
- Small stones: fill a coffee can
- Ivory Liquid

INSTALLATION

1. To position indoor garden: Choose a prominent window for your garden. Ideal locations could include entryway, living room, kitchen, or library. Note exposure and leave a thermometer there for a few days to ascertain temperatures.

2. Move chosen table or bench to window position.

3. Floor protection: Water can damage floors. Tile, stone, and linoleum floors are generally safe from splashes and spills. Carpet or wood floors under an indoor garden must be protected from water. Lay heavy plastic sheeting underneath the entire table. Hide plastic with absorbent washable rugs such as cotton rag. Occasionally check the floor underneath the garden table and wash the rug as needed.

4. Purchase plants as per the sun exposure, temperature, and general humidity provided. Buy at least 5 plants to begin your garden.

5. Transplant all plants into decorative containers as per directions in "Contain Yourself" on page 153.

6. Keep transplanted material out of direct sun for three days.

7. To arrange your indoor garden: Position potted plants as you would in an outdoor garden. Avoid the expected: Placing tallest plant off-center at the rear or as a corner anchor sometimes looks better than the usual rear center position.

8. Underneath pots: Use china platters, plates, and saucers instead of usual pottery saucers. Old-fashioned metal serving trays can hold several plants. These provide extra protection from water stains and can be purchased at flea markets.

9. To provide height: Use an overturned pot like a small stage. Set potted plant on top. This works very well with plants like begonias or ferns that drape or have a curved posture.

10. Trailing vines: A trailing plant like ivy can cascade out of its own pot, down the edge of an overturned pot, and be fanned out among other plants.

11. Climbing vines: Use very small nails and string to train climbers

upward and make a living frame around the window. Jasmine and climbing onion will climb strings.

12. To add decorative elements: Arrange ornamental objects on the plant table. A small table lamp will light up this area after dark. Small votives add a festive touch when entertaining. Be sure to keep electrical devices away from water.

13. To increase humidity: Place bowls of water on plant table for extra humidity. Seashells or decorative stones can be placed in the water if desired. Keep water topped up and clean.

14. To circulate air: Use a small inexpensive fan to circulate air. Set on floor and tilt upward and away from plants. Do not blow air directly on plants, as this will dry out flowers and leaves.

15. Indoor garden maintenance: Avoid overwatering. Poke finger into soil to check for moisture. If completely dry, water according to nursery instructions. Apply water gently with small long-spouted watering can to avoid splashing soil away from surface roots.

16. Do not let pots sit in water. Remove water that drains into saucers, etc., underneath pots so that containers never sit in water.

17. For containers without holes: If using a cachepot with no drainage hole, make sure that the inner pot does not sit in water contained in the cachepot.

18. To fertilize: Avoid overfertilizing. Mix a weak solution of bloom booster plant fertilizer in an empty gallon milk jug. If directions say use 1 teaspoon of granules per gallon water, use ¼ teaspoon. Mark this jug with "BB" for "bloom booster."

19. In the second gallon jug, mix a weak solution of regular plant fertilizer as per instructions above. Regular plant fertilizer promotes leaf growth. This jug can be marked "REG."

20. Do not apply fertilizer solution to dry plants. If necessary, water first.

21. Fertilize "weekly, weakly." Choose the same day of the week for ease of remembering (for example, "Fertilize on Fridays"). On even-numbered Fridays, use the bloom booster. On odd Fridays, use

regular solution. On the last Friday of the month, do not fertilize.

22. To apply fertilizer, pour solution from the milk jug into a small, long-spouted watering can. Pour on soil. Allow to drain and remove liquid from saucers as usual.

23. Store extra fertilizer in jugs for next application.

24. If possible, store all indoor garden supplies together in a galvanized washtub or other large container to keep them organized and handy.

25. Groom plants as needed. Remove yellow foliage with sharp scissors. Deadhead spent flowers. Keep soil surface and containers tidy. If wet soil spills on the table, allow water to dry and blow away soil. Wiping wet soil creates streaks.

26. Watch for white fly, spider mites, scale, and other harmful bugs that may attack your indoor plants. At first sign, remove the afflicted plant from the garden and isolate in another room.

27. Fill plant sprayer with warm water and 2 drops of Ivory Liquid soap. In my experience, this mixture will cure all bug ills.

28. Place buggy plant in kitchen sink and spray with soap solution until every leaf is drenched. Leave plant in sink for half hour, then rinse thoroughly with clean water from the sprayer attachment. Keep affected plant away from other plants.

29. Check plant daily for reappearance of bugs. Bugs will appear until all eggs previously laid have hatched. Spray at least every 3 days, or more often as needed.

30. Keep affected plant watered, but do not apply fertilizer.

31. When no bugs are seen for 2 weeks, replace plant in table garden and resume normal fertilizing schedule.

32. OPTIONAL: If possible, place your tabletop garden outside in the shade for summer. Do not do this until night temperatures stay above 60 degrees. Remove rug and plastic sheeting and air out floor indoors if possible. Reassemble indoor garden before frost. Don't be concerned if your plants pout when they're moved back indoors. This is natural.

PLANT HARDINESS ZONES

1	Below –50°F.
2	–50° to –40°
3	–40° to –30°
4	–30° to –20°
5	–20° to –10°
6	–10° to 0°
7	0° to 10°
8	10° to 20°
9	20° to 30°
10	30° to 40°
11	Above 40°

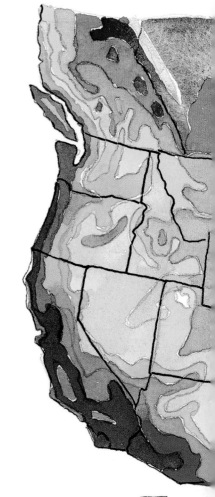

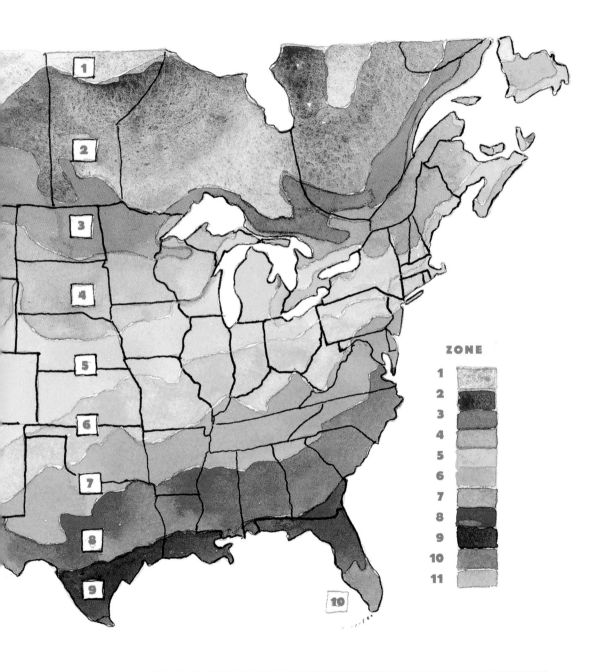

ZONE

1
2
3
4
5
6
7
8
9
10
11

INDEX